you called me WHAT?

THE  GUIDE TO
CELEBRITY BABY NAMES

JOHN PERRY

Published in 2006 by HarperCollins*Publishers*

HarperCollins *Publishers*
77-85 Fulham Palace Road
London W6 8JB

www.collins.co.uk

© The Sun, News Group Newspapers Ltd, 2006

Reprint   10   9   8   7   6   5   4   3   2   1   0

The Sun and *Sun* are registered trademarks of News Group Newspapers Ltd

ISBN-13   978-0-00-722849-2
ISBN-10   0-00-722849-X

British Library Cataloguing in Publication Data
A catalogue record for this book is available from the British Library.

Design: Valle Walkley
Printed and bound in Great Britain by Clays Ltd, St Ives plc.

Contents

FOR *Jack* AND *Tom*

(with apologies for a woeful lack of imagination)

Blame Frank

FRANK Zappa started it.

Stars had given their kids mildly exotic names before, but nothing like Frank's. The moment the eccentric rocker dubbed his first daughter Moon Unit in 1967 he began a celebrity craze for barmy baby names which, almost 40 years on, shows no signs of abating.

These days few self-respecting celebs would dare name their child anything 'ordinary'. The Top 10 baby names chosen by millions of lesser mortals across Britain and America don't stand an earthly chance.

For a star, no name is beyond consideration. Children can be superheroes, song lyrics, household objects, cities, countries, sportsmen, musicians, seasons, animals, modes of transport or even fellow celebs. They can be called CrimeFighter or Pirate without looking out of place among other celebrity offspring.

Each new name triggers a chorus of disapproval from ordinary folk. 'It's child abuse', critics say, 'The kid is an open goal for bullies.' And of course they have a point. But before we get carried away with indignation, let's remember that while a few celebrity children HAVE changed their names, none has yet jumped from a building shouting: 'They shouldn't have called me Rainbow Moonchild!'

Why they do it

Before we get to the nutty names celebs give their kids, we must ask the crucial question: WHY?

Clearly, the world would be a dull place if all boys were Jack and Daniel and all girls Emily and Lucy. But what possesses even the most level-headed star to saddle their sprogs with names that could expose them to ridicule?

The obvious answer is that they want the child to stand out from the pack, just as they perceive they do themselves. Some want their kids to share their celebrity, says psychologist Susan Quilliam. 'They can't resist the need for them to be seen as different from ordinary people's kids.'

Another child psychologist, Dr Pat Spungin, says: 'In celebrity culture, it's "I'm special so my child must be special – they can't have a name like everyone else".'

Professor Lewis Lipsitt, a US expert in human development, believes some stars want their offspring to stand out independently of their fame. An unusual name is a chance for the kid 'to be distinctive in their own right instead of just being known as a celebrity's child'.

Nearly all the experts fear such names make the child vulnerable to bullying. Psychologist Dr Jack Boyle says: 'Children look for something to mock other children about and giving your child an absurd name is one way of singling them out for bullying.'

Another psychologist, Cynthia McVey, adds: 'It can be selfish to give a child a name which stands out too much.'

The effect probably depends on the child, though. Child psychologist Angela Lyons says: 'I knew one boy who was very proud of his name Valentine and he took a lot of teasing. It was part of his strength of character.'

As for the celebrity trend for cutesy girls' names (such as Jamie Oliver's Daisy Boo and Poppy Honey), Dr Spungin has this advice: 'When she's a woman in her forties those names don't quite work the same.

'My advice is to name a child so that if they are sitting on the Bank of England's monetary committee they have a name that'll be taken seriously.'

Which rules out a great many of the ones you're about to encounter.

Your
A-Z
guide

Some of the 500 or so names here are truly bonkers, but by no means all. Some are bold, others beautiful. A small number are not even that unusual – they may just have an interesting story attached. Not all the meanings or motivations behind them are known – so, with tongue in cheek, we have made a guess. Generally, if both parents are famous, they're both listed. Otherwise not. Siblings with equally bizarre or noteworthy names are also listed, so you can track a theme running through the family, or not, as the case may be.

Our suggested alternatives which the celebs should have considered are either an even more absurd variation of the chosen name or one that seems to chime with the celeb's surname (or the child's, if different). Sometimes they may be a (possibly obscure) reference to the celeb's life or career. Have fun working them out.

A

FROM *Ace* TO *Avalon*

Ace   NATALIE APPLETON & LIAM HOWLETT

Are the All Saint and the Prodigy star tennis fans? If so, this is a perfect name for their little smasher.

> ***Should have considered:*** Lob

Adria   TOM PETTY

The rock star's film-maker daughter seems to be a consonant or two short of a real name. But hey, Anything That's Rock And Roll's fine.

> ***Should have considered:*** Betty

Agnes   THOM YORKE

Derives from the Greek for 'pure' or 'chaste'. The movie *Agnes of God* could be written for her – her dad being the godlike Radiohead frontman. SEE ALSO: *Noah*.

> ***Should have considered:*** Björk

Ahmet Emuukha Rodan   FRANK ZAPPA

Debate rages over the origin of the second Zappa son's name. It is thought the eccentric rock genius named him after Ahmet Ertegun, once president of Atlantic Records – or after an imaginary servant Frank and his wife used to pretend served them tea at home. Rodan is a monster in a Japanese movie franchise. SEE ALSO: *Diva Muffin, Dweezil, Moon Unit*.

> ***Should have considered:*** Godzilla

Aja Louise   MITCH DORGE

Baffling little number from the drummer with the Crash Test Dummies. Perhaps he often leaves the door open.

> ***Should have considered:*** Georgia

Alaia

STEPHEN BALDWIN

Imagine the lip the *Usual Suspects* star will get when she's older. 'Dad, are you calling me Alaia?' In fact, it's an Arabic name meaning 'sublime'.

> ***Should have considered:*** *Afibba*

Alessandra

ANDY GARCIA

Beautiful girl's name from the Cuban star of *Godfather III* and *Things to Do in Denver When You're Dead*. Or should that be dad?

> ***Should have considered:*** *Geri*

Alexa

TROY AIKMAN

The legendary quarterback for the three-times Superbowl-winning Dallas Cowboys of the 1990s opted for the short form of Alexandra. It's from the Greek for 'to defend'. Which wasn't Troy's game.

> ***Should have considered:*** *Touchdown*

Alexa Rae

BILLY JOEL & CHRISTIE BRINKLEY

The Piano Man and his Uptown Girl named their daughter this, then sadly parted company. Guess that's just the way they were.

> ***Should have considered:*** *Betty Ford*

Alisabeth

TYNE DALY

The *Cagney and Lacey* star loves to tinker with the vowels in common names. Two more examples later. Judging Emy, anyone? SEE ALSO: *Alyxandra, Kathryne*.

> ***Should have considered:*** *Adith, Adna*

Allegra Sky
JOHN LEGUIZAMO

The fast-talking Colombian star of *Carlito's Way* is also a comic, and is guaranteed a laugh here. In Latin, Allegra means 'cheerful' and 'full of energy'. And Sky? A tribute to the satellite broadcaster?

Should have considered: Cloudy, Blue

Alphonse
MORGAN FREEMAN

This means 'noble and ready', neither of which described America's most famous Alphonse – Capone. Let's hope movie star Morgan won't remain Unforgiven for it. SEE ALSO: *Deena, Morgana, Saifoulaye.*

Should have considered: Gotti, Gambino

Alyxandra
TYNE DALY

Here she goes again, tweaking those kids' vowels. Not for *Judging Amy* star Tyne the bog standard 'Alexandra'. Oh no. SEE ALSO: *Alisabeth, Kathryne.*

Should have considered: Ymma

Amandine
JOHN MALKOVICH

Crazy name, crazy guy. The quirky star of *Dangerous Liaisons* and *In the Line of Fire* chose a derivation of Amanda, Latin for 'beloved'. SEE ALSO: *Loewy.*

Should have considered: Amandela, Amandoolah

Amba
JADE JAGGER

Mick's a Rolling Stone, Jade's a gemstone and now little Amba is too. At least, Amber is. And mum's a jewellery designer. So that must be the connection. SEE ALSO: *Assisi.*

Should have considered: Lapis Lazuli

Amber Rose
SIMON & YASMIN LE BON 😊

An old fossil of a name from the Duran Duran veteran and his supermodel missus. Actually, Amber's now in the top 50 girls' names in Britain. And Amber Nectar must always be a temptation for dads. SEE ALSO: *Saffron Sahara, Tallulah Pine.*

Should have considered: Bonnie

Aminta
PETE TOWNSHEND 😊

You've called me Who?

Should have considered: Quadrophelia

Amirah
SHAQUILLE O'NEAL 😊

On reflection, Amirah is a lovely name the basketball genius picked for his daughter. It means 'princess' in Hebrew. Here's looking at you, kid. SEE ALSO: *Shaquir, Shareef, Taahirah.*

Should have considered: Tatum

Anais
NOEL GALLAGHER & MEG MATHEWS 😊

So, What's The Story? Oasis songwriter Noel named his daughter after Anais Nin, the French erotic writer who was his then wife's favourite.

Should have considered: Liamme

Annaliza
STEVEN SEAGAL & KELLY LEBROCK 😊

Few would argue with the choice of the hardman star who is at once Hard To Kill, Marked For Death and Out For Justice. SEE ALSO: *Arrisa, Domenick, Justice.*

Should have considered: Kittiwake

Anton

AL PACINO & BEVERLEY D'ANGELO

Arguably the world's greatest actor picked the German and Russian form of Anthony. And presumably he announced at the Christening: 'Say hello to my lil' friend!'

Should have considered: *Serpico, Carlito*

Anya

TOM HULCE

Who knows why the Oscar-nominated star of *Amadeus* picked this? Of course, he was also in *National Lampoon's Animal House*. Could it be *National Lampoon's* Anya Hulce? Surely not.

Should have considered: *Dulcie*

Apple

GWYNETH PALTROW & CHRIS MARTIN

The actress and the Coldplay singer thought it was a-peeling ... most people thought it was appalling. Poor Apple's only hope at school is if the bullies are Banana and Mango.

Should have considered: *Pippa*

Aquinnah

MICHAEL J FOX & TRACY POLLAN

Tracy's surname is not to be sneezed at, but we digress. Aquinnah is named after a tiny town on Martha's Vineyard, Massachusetts, where the *Back to the Future* star and his wife go on holiday.

Should have considered: *Orlando*

Arnelle

O J SIMPSON

The American football legend and actor (real name Orenthal James Simpson) – now most famous for being cleared of a double murder – picked this derivation of Arnold back in the 1960s.

Should have considered: *Marge*

Arpad Flynn

ELLE MACPHERSON

The Aussie supermodel known as 'The Body' has an excuse – the lad's father is Swiss financier Arpad Busson. Arpad means 'wanderer' in Hungarian. Which became apt when Elle and Arpad went separate ways in 2005. SEE ALSO: *Aurelius Cy*.

> **Should have considered:** Double Decker

Arrisa

STEVEN SEAGAL & KELLY LEBROCK

Her mum uttered the immortal phrase in a Pantene ad: 'Don't hate me because I'm beautiful.' OK mum, I won't hate you for that. SEE ALSO: *Annaliza, Domenick, Justice*.

> **Should have considered:** Flocka

Arun

THE EDGE

Arun got off lightly, given that her dad has spent most of his life under a dodgy pseudonym. The U2 guitarist, real name Dave Evans, must have told the missus: 'I'm having the name Arun With Or Without You.' SEE ALSO: *Blue Angel, Hollee, Levi*.

> **Should have considered:** Stairway Tu

Assisi

JADE JAGGER

Mick and Bianca's daughter (Jade Sheena Jezebel Jagger to be precise) paid tribute to the Italian town with her first daughter. Lucky Assisi wasn't a boy! SEE ALSO: *Amba*.

> **Should have considered:** Florence

Astrella Celeste

DONOVAN

The British singer/songwriter, full name Donovan Philips Leitch, had two little stars with heavenly-sounding names in the 1970s.

Astrella got the nicest. Pity poor Oriole Nebula (see separate entry).
SEE ALSO: *Ione Skye*.

Should have considered: *Sputnik 2*

Atherton Grace DON JOHNSON 😌

Never figured the *Miami Vice* star for a cricket fan and few would
credit Michael Atherton with grace. But who can forget his 185 not
out at Jo'burg in 1996? Not Don, obviously. A moving tribute to
Athers? Erm, possibly not. SEE ALSO: *Jasper Breckenridge*.

Should have considered: *Gooch*

Atlanta Noo JOHN TAYLOR & AMANDA DE CADENET 😌

Atlanta's a city in Georgia. So far so good. Noo? Short for Noodlehead,
a nickname the Duran Duran bassist and the former wild child had
for each other. It was probably funny at the time.

Should have considered: *Hunny bunny*

Atticus TONY ADAMS 🙂

Top name, especially from an Arsenal legend of lofty stature. It means
'from Athens' and was famously used for Atticus Finch, the lawyer in
To Kill a Mockingbird.

Should have considered: *Grizzly*

Auden NOAH WYLE 😌

ER's Dr Carter paid tribute to the great British poet W H Auden,
whose works include the famous 'Funeral Blues' read out during
Four Weddings and a Funeral.

Should have considered: *Wordsworth*

Audice

ADRIAN BELEW

Little excuse for this made-up moniker from the King Crimson guitarist. Let's hope she's not crimson with embarrassment.

Should have considered: Lookout

Audio Science

SHANNYN SOSSAMAN

This horror from the *Knight's Tale* actress (full name Shannon Marie Kahoolani Sossamon) is of the Frank Zappa school (see Ahmet *et al.*). Who knows what possessed her? Shannyn is a part-time DJ ... maybe she's picky about her hi-fi sound.

Should have considered: Auxilliary Out

Aurelius Cy

ELLE MACPHERSON

From the Latin 'golden', this is supermodel Elle's second golden boy. The perfect name ... should he grow up to be Emperor of ancient Rome. SEE ALSO: *Arpad Flynn*.

Should have considered: Haley Caesar

Autumn

FOREST WHITAKER

Leaf it out! The American star of *Bird* and *Panic Room* loves 'nature' names, as further entries will reveal. Guess you might too, if you'd spent life as a Forest. But to be fair, this is his stepdaughter, so he didn't actually pick this one. SEE ALSO: *Ocean, Sonnet, True*.

Should have considered: n/a (Not his choice)

Avalon

MIKE KROEGER

The guitarist with Canadian rockers Nickelback landed on the mythical British isle when he picked his daughter's name.

Should have considered: Atlantis

B

FROM *Bailey* TO *Buck*

Bailey

ANTHONY EDWARDS

Dr Mark Greene on *ER* picked a common surname as his son's first name. It derives from the word 'bailiff', the term for a minor official. Or perhaps he's fond of the creamy Irish tipple. SEE ALSO: *Esme, Wallis*.

Should have considered: Edward, of course

Bamboo

BIG BOI

Mr Boi is the Outkast hip-hop star whose real name is Antwan Andre Patton. Let's hope kids not named after woody perennials don't make his poor lad an outcast at school. SEE ALSO: *Cross*.

Should have considered: Knitting

Banjo

RACHEL GRIFFITHS

The Aussie actress from TV's *Six Feet Under* and movies including *Muriel's Wedding* chose the perfect name ... for any son of Joe Strummer. Sadly Joe wasn't the dad.

Should have considered: Ukelele

Barriana

BARRY WHITE

Sorry Baz ... but Barry, or forms of it, do not a girl's name make. Nonetheless, the legendary soul singer, dubbed the 'Walrus of Love', gave it a go anyway.

Should have considered: Barriareef

Baylee

BRIAN LITTRELL

Just a theory: in newspapers a 'literal' is a spelling mistake. Was Backstreet Boys singer Brian LITTRELL trying in vain to spell Bailey?

Should have considered: Bayli, Bail-E

Beau Devin

DAVID CASSIDY

A French-Gaelic combo was the former teenage pop heart-throb's choice. Beau means 'handsome', which millions of teenage girls certainly thought his dad was.

Should have considered: *Butch*

Bebe Orleans

NUNO BETTENCOURT

A baby called Bebe? Or is she 'Beeb'? Apparently the Extreme guitar virtuoso and his wife spent a fortnight rejecting 'meaningless' names before landing on this. SEE ALSO: *Lorenzo Aureolino.*

Should have considered: *A while longer*

Bechet Dumaine

WOODY ALLEN & SOON-YI PREVIN

The jazz-loving movie-maker honoured two New Orleans legends, clarinetist Sidney Bechet and cornet player Louis Dumaine. So the child's a one-woman band.

Should have considered: *Louise Armstrong*

Beckett

MALCOLM MCDOWELL

Presumably the *Clockwork Orange* star named his son after the playwright Samuel Beckett, so it's tempting to call it a Krapp name, but actually it's quite cool.

Should have considered: *Godot*

Bella

BILLY BOB THORNTON

Bella, Billy. Billy, Bella. A beautiful choice from the star of *Monster's Ball* and many others.

Should have considered: *Bella Bub*

Betty Kitten

JONATHAN ROSS & JANE GOLDMAN

Yep, fine while the lass is under ten. But can you see her striding into a business meeting in a power suit with Betty Kitten on her name tag? At least, for her TV presenter dad's sake, it doesn't have an 'r' in it. SEE ALSO: *Honey Kinney, Harvey Kirby*.

Should have considered: *Wachel, Webecca, etc.*

Bibi Belle

ANNA RYDER RICHARDSON

Alliteration is clearly completely crucial to Ms R-R, star of *Changing Rooms* and *House Invaders*. But in case you thought Bibi was made up, it means 'king's daughter' in East Africa. SEE ALSO: *Dixie Dot*.

Should have considered: *Bow Bell*

Blossom

KACEY AINSWORTH

Another cutesy 'little girl' name, this from *EastEnders*' Little Mo. She reportedly made the decision after talking to Gwyneth Paltrow at an antenatal class. Indeed, Blossom's only hope is to form a gang with Gwyn's Apple to fight off the bullies.

Should have considered: *Bud*

Blue Angel

THE EDGE

Imagine the siblings chatting in guitarist Dave Evans' house: 'I've got a funny name.' 'U2?' SEE ALSO: *Arun, Hollee, Levi*.

Should have considered: *Red Devil*

Bo

ULRIKA JONSSON

The Swedish TV girl named her daughter after her dad. It's a boy's name, but, hey, it's sweet enough for a girl. SEE ALSO: *Martha Sky Hope*.

Should have considered: *Magic*

Bobbi Kristina   BOBBY BROWN & WHITNEY HOUSTON 😊

Hats off to Bobby and Whitney for imagination. Not! Imagine poor Whitney's confusion. Which Bobbi/Bobby is it? 'How Will I Know?' she warbles.

Should have considered: *Golden*

Bobby Jack   JADE GOODY & JEFF BRAZIER 😊

Two diminutives from the lovable Big Brother motormouth.

Should have considered: *Kebab*

Boman   MATTHEW MODINE 😊

Granted, Boman Modine has a certain ring to it but what IS a Boman? An archer? Was *Full Metal Jacket*'s Private Joker having a private joke?

Should have considered: *Mo*

Bonnie Blue   BILLY IDOL 😊

Bonnie can thank her lucky stars she's got a more sensible name than the one her old man's been sporting for 30 years. The faux punk is really William Michael Albert Broad, by the way. SEE ALSO: *Willem Wolfe*.

Should have considered: *Surf*

Boston   KURT RUSSELL 😊

Go figure. The man who escaped from New York and LA called his son Boston. Let's hope he never makes 'Escape from Boston', or relations may be strained.

Should have considered: *Russell*

Braison

BILLY RAY CYRUS

Bizarre creation from the 'Achy Breaky Heart' singer. Was he aiming for B-Ray-Son? That would be brazen stupidity.

Should have considered: Billson

Brandi

ROSEANNE BARR

The TV comedienne is the Barr that served up a Brandi. SEE ALSO: *Buck*.

Should have considered: Cocktail

Brawley

NICK NOLTE

It may look like the hell-raising *48 Hours* star picked a name meaning 'has tendency to fight'. But it's actually an old English name meaning 'from a hillside meadow'. Brawley and his dad share the middle name King – Nolte's mother's maiden name.

Should have considered: Knuckles

Bria

EDDIE MURPHY

Cheesy offering from the man who made his name in *48 Hours* with Nick Nolte (see Brawley, above). This is a distant variation of Bridget. SEE ALSO: *Shane, Zola*.

Should have considered: Chedda

Brooklyn

DAVID & VICTORIA BECKHAM

The Becks' eldest boy was famously named after the New York borough where he was conceived. Lucky they weren't in Queens. SEE ALSO: *Cruz, Romeo*.

Should have considered: Bognor

Bruno

NIGELLA LAWSON

Colour is a common theme for the domestic goddess – Bruno means 'brown' and her own name is Latin for 'small and black'. SEE ALSO: *Cosima*.

> ***Should have considered:*** *Indigo*

Bryce Dallas

RON HOWARD

The *Happy Days* star turned film director conceived her in Dallas and named her after Bryce Canyon, a formation of red rocks in Utah, which match his daughter's hair. SEE ALSO: *Paige Carlyle, Reed*.

> ***Should have considered:*** *Fire Engine Dallas*

Buck

ROSEANNE BARR

She certainly made a few bucks as TV's favourite comedienne and this was another. SEE ALSO: *Brandi*.

> ***Should have considered:*** *Noodle*

C

FROM *Caleb* TO *Cydney*

Caleb

JACK NICHOLSON 😊

The Shining star and Susan Anspach picked a Hebrew name meaning 'devotion to God'. Shame he decided against John. Think how much fun he could have had saying 'Heeeere's Johnny!'

Should have considered: *Nick*

Caley Leigh

CHEVY CHASE 😊

Chevy, or Cornelius Crane Chase as he started life, gave his daughter the male spelling of Kayleigh. Caley Leigh? Surely-ly not! SEE ALSO: *Cydney Cathalene.*

Should have considered: *Steeple*

Cali Tee

JAMES HETFIELD 😊

This strange brew from the Metallica frontman isn't everyone's cuppa, but each to their own.

Should have considered: *Potter Tee*

Calico

ALICE COOPER 😊

Why would a dad name his son after a type of cloth? Who knows? But when the dad is Vincent Damon Furnier, and he's spent his life as a rock star called Alice, expect a few surprises.

Should have considered: *Alison*

Calista

DAVID CARRADINE 😊

Not that unusual now, since Calista Flockhart became a star in *Ally McBeal*. Besides, who's going to argue with Caine from *Kung Fu*? SEE ALSO: *Free, Kansas.*

Should have considered: *Carrie*

Camera

ARTHUR ASHE

Sadly, the American tennis legend is no longer around to explain why he named his daughter after an item of photographic equipment. Perhaps she was pretty as a picture.

Should have considered: *Lenscappe*

Carmen

ROBERT PLANT

The Led Zeppelin singer's choice is a derivation of the Spanish word for garden, a popular place for Plants. SEE ALSO: *Logan Romero*.

Should have considered: *Yucca*

Carnie

BRIAN WILSON

Why the gifted Beach Boy picked this God Only Knows.

Should have considered: *Barbara Ann*

Cash

SLASH

This is obviously something dear to the heart of the Guns 'n' Roses guitarist, real name Saul Hudson. Or was it for Johnny Cash? SEE ALSO: *London Emilio*.

Should have considered: *Luka*

Cashel Blake

DANIEL DAY-LEWIS

Cashel is an Irish name meaning 'loving'. Daniel, star of *Gangs of New York* and many others, was born Daniel Michael Blake Day-Lewis. So Blake was In The Name Of The Father. SEE ALSO: *Gabriel-Kane*.

Should have considered: *Lou*

Caspar
CLAUDIA SCHIFFER & MATTHEW VAUGHN ☺

A little treasure for the supermodel and the film director (real name Matthew De Vere Drummond) – and 'treasure' is what it means in its original Persian.

Should have considered: Bulldog

Cassius
DAMIEN HIRST ☺

This goes back to the Romans, Cassius being one of Caesar's assassins. But maybe the controversial artist is a fan of Muhammad Ali, born Cassius Clay.

Should have considered: Brutus

Castor Virgil
JAMES HETFIELD ☺

The Metallica frontman seems an unlikely classical scholar, but Castor was Helen of Troy's brother and Virgil the Roman poet who wrote about the sacking of the city.

Should have considered: Homer

Chadwick
STEVE McQUEEN ☺

It's a surname, really … an old English word meaning 'from the warrior's town'. *The Magnificent Seven* icon probably just thought it sounded cool.

Should have considered: Godsave

Chance
PAUL HOGAN ☺

Its original meaning is 'good fortune'. Doubt the *Crocodile Dundee* star's son counts himself lucky, though.

Should have considered: Hulk

Chance Armstrong

LARRY KING

See previous entry for 'Chance'. Was CNN host Larry honouring cycling legend Lance with the middle name?

Should have considered: Burger

Chandrika

CHRIS SQUIRE

It's a mystery why the bass player with Yes dreamed this up. But at the time the band was recording prog rock horror 'Tales from Topographic Oceans', so anything was possible.

Should have considered: Male Voi

Chanel

NELLY

The hip-hop star, real name Cornell Haynes Jr, named his daughter after perfume. Eau dear, eau dear.

Should have considered: Dior

Chastity

CHER & SONNY BONO

The singer and actress, real name Cherilyn Sarkasian La Peir, placed high expectations on her daughter here. Especially considering one of her schoolmates was Experience (two others were Eureka and Breeze … well, it was the Sixties). Chastity became a lesbian.

Should have considered: Yoko

Cherish

CHARLENE TILTON

Presumably Lucy Ewing from TV's *Dallas* was indicating her daughter would be cherished. Either that or she wanted her to be Cher-ish … i.e. prance around in Spandex into her fifties.

Should have considered: Paris

Chiani

BOON GOULD 🐱

The Level 42 guitarist was born Rowland, so made-up names are Running In The Family.

Should have considered: Bobbi

China

GRACE SLICK 🐱

The Jefferson Airplane/Starship singer was long said to have named her daughter God with a small 'g' – 'because we want her to be humble'. This was actually just a joke to a nurse in the maternity room. As presumably was China. But the poor girl was stuck with that.

Should have considered: Oil

Chudney

DIANA ROSS 🐱

Stunningly daft choice from the music legend. Unsurprisingly, no meaning can be found for Chudney. Chutney, however, is a sweet and spicy condiment. SEE ALSO: *Ross*.

Should have considered: Peanud Budder

Chynna

MICHELLE PHILLIPS 🐱

The Mamas and Papas singer obviously discounted plain old China. Her exotically-spelled daughter grew up to become a star herself, then married actor Billy Baldwin.

Should have considered: Syngapora

Cicely

SANDRA BERNHARD 🐱

Not Cecily, you understand, Cicely. But then bisexual comic actress Sandra – Madonna's pal – has always been the sort wild enough to go crazy with vowels.

Should have considered: Modanna

Clementine
CLAUDIA SCHIFFER & MATTHEW VAUGHN

Oh my darling, what a fruity name. Actually it's a nice one, this – don't let those other kids take the pith.

Should have considered: *Satsuma*

Coco
COURTENEY COX & DAVID ARQUETTE

A famous clown's name, which in this case came from the nickname Mama Coco, given to Courteney's mum when the *Friends* star was a kid.

Should have considered: *Krusty*

Colton
CHRIS EVERT

In old English it means 'from the dark town'. The one-time tennis golden girl chose it for her youngest son. And isn't it a smasher?

Should have considered: *Connors*

Columbus
LADY HELEN & TIM TAYLOR

Three theories sprang up: the 26th in line to the throne was named after explorer Christopher Columbus; a Knightsbridge restaurant the couple liked; or a dog called Columbus owned by her dad, the Duke of Kent. The couple never explained.

Should have considered: *Pizza Hut*

Cooper
PHILIP SEYMOUR HOFFMAN

A cooper is a barrel-maker. Only the cruellest person would say the star of *Magnolia* and *Boogie Nights* is himself slightly barrel-esque.

Should have considered: *Dustin*

Corde

The rap star, real name Calvin Cordozar Broadus, took a derivation of his middle name for his first son. And we don't mean his middle name is 'Doggy'. SEE ALSO: *Cordell*.

Should have considered: Pup

Cordell

SNOOP DOGG

Way to go, Snoop ... just add two consonants for a whole new name! This one, for Mr Dogg's second son, at least has a meaning – it's Latin for 'small rope'. SEE ALSO: *Corde*.

Should have considered: Cordtina

Corey

SUZANNE SHAW & DARREN DAY

The choice of the ex-Hearsay singer and the TV love rat has various meanings from 'chosen' to 'ravine'. Corey and Apple Martin should meet.

Should have considered: Sandy

Cosima

NIGELLA LAWSON

A Greek name meaning 'order' from the domestic goddess. Which aptly describes the state of her pantry. SEE ALSO: *Bruno*.

Should have considered: Cupcake

Cosimo

BECK & MARISSA RIBISI

The male version of Cosima, from musician Beck Hansen and his actress wife.

Should have considered: Alan

Cosma Shiva

The eccentric New Wave singer picked a Greek-Indian mix, Shiva being the Indian god, Cosma meaning 'of the universe'.

> **Should have considered:** *Van*

Crispian
HAYLEY MILLS

Crispin means 'curly-haired' but the actress added an 'a' for reasons known only to herself. Her son became a rock musician in Kula Shaker.

> **Should have considered:** *Bob*

Cross
BIG BOI

The Outkast hip-hop star (Antwan Andre Patton) may fall out with his son over this. The lad's bound to be cross when he's a big boy. SEE ALSO: *Bamboo*.

> **Should have considered:** *General*

Cruz
DAVID & VICTORIA BECKHAM

This means 'cross' in Spanish – but it's usually a girl's name or a surname. The Beckhams were reported to want a 'holy' name for child No. 3. But maybe it had as much to do with Becks' trademark, the pinpoint cross. SEE ALSO: *Brooklyn, Romeo*.

> **Should have considered:** *Nutmeg (Nuez Moscada in Spanish)*

Cydney Cathalene
CHEVY CHASE

National Lampooner Chevy is a fan of this stock celeb trick – pepping up ordinary names by mangling the spelling. SEE ALSO: *Caley Leigh*.

> **Should have considered:** *Sharyn, Tracee*

FROM *Daemon* TO *Dylan*

Daemon

Granted, the lead singer with Slayer was unlikely to pick Colin or Simon. But Daemon? What the devil was he thinking? The poor lad's marked for life … by the number of the Beast.

Should have considered: *Beelzebub*

Daisy Boo

JAMIE OLIVER

Daisy, fair enough. But Boo? It's the TV chef's nickname for wife Jools. But why condemn the kid to a childhood of having friends jump out from hedges yelling 'Boo!'? SEE ALSO: *Poppy Honey*.

Should have considered: *Watchout!*

Dakota Mayi

DON JOHNSON & MELANIE GRIFFITH

Cool Native American name for the daughter of *Miami Vice*'s Don and *Working Girl* star Melanie Griffith, later to wed Antonio Banderas.

Should have considered: *Sioux*

Dalton

LINDA HAMILTON & BRUCE ABBOTT

This apparently means 'from the town in the dale'. Maybe the *Terminator* star and her actor ex are *Emmerdale* fans.

Should have considered: *Russ*

Damian

LIZ HURLEY & STEVE BING

Not that unusual before 1976 – but who called their son Damian after *The Omen*? A name guaranteed to cause horrible deaths and scare baboons.

Should have considered: *Lucifer*

Dandelion

KEITH RICHARDS

This hippy-era name, from a 1967 Rolling Stones song Keef wrote with Mick Jagger, was far from fine and dandy with its owner, who later became plain Angela.

Should have considered: Angela

Dariel

JON PERTWEE

The origin of this is lost in the mists of time, like the third Dr Who himself.

Should have considered: Tardisa

Dashiell

CATE BLANCHETT

Lord of the Rings' elf queen Galadriel was inspired by Dashiell Hammett, American author of crime novels including *The Maltese Falcon*. SEE ALSO: *Roman*.

Should have considered: Elrond

Deacon

REESE WITHERSPOON

An ecclesiastical name from the *Legally Blonde* star, virtually guaranteeing her son a career in the Church.

Should have considered: Cardinal

Deana

DEAN MARTIN

Not an overwhelming amount of imagination from the Rat Pack actor, simply adding 'a' to his own name.

Should have considered: Martini

Declyn

Girls Just Wanna Have Fun with the spelling of their babies' names, so here's a variant of the Irish Saint Declan.

Should have considered: *Patryck*

Deena

Maybe it's the female derivation of the Jewish name Deen. Maybe the *Shawshank Redemption* star simply made it up. SEE ALSO: *Alphonse, Morgana, Saifoulaye.*

Should have considered: *Freeda*

Dekker

NiKKi, SiXX. DeKKer. You get the idea. The Motley Crüe bassist, born Frank Carlton Serafino Ferranna, prefers his consonants hard and two at a time. Like his women. SEE ALSO: *Gunner, Storm Brieanne.*

Should have considered: *Lukky*

Delphine

This could mean 'woman of Delphi'. But, given that The Band singer's daughter was born during the 'flower power' era just before Woodstock, it's probably to do with the plant Delphinium.

Should have considered: *Dandelion. Perhaps not (see Dandelion)*

Deni Montana

Probably doesn't seem a crazy name when you've dated Moon Zappa, like *Cheers* star Woody.

Should have considered: *Harriet*

Denim

TONI BRAXTON 😊

The Grammy-winning singer of 'Unbreak My Heart' stitched up her son with a type of jeans material. SEE ALSO: *Diezel*.

> **Should have considered:** *Gene*

Destry

STEVEN SPIELBERG & KATE CAPSHAW 😊

A movie name from the most successful director of all. Jimmy Stewart played Destry in *Destry Rides Again*, though Spielberg's Destry, oddly, is a girl. SEE ALSO: *Mikaela, Sawyer*.

> **Should have considered:** *Liberty Valance*

Deva

MONICA BELLUCCI 😊

The Matrix star's daughter is 'superior' in Hindi or 'divine' in Celtic. Neither is likely to keep her feet on the ground.

> **Should have considered:** *Trinity*

Devin

DENIS LEARY 😊

A Celtic name meaning 'poet' – and a boy's name at that – but comic Denis has done madder things.

> **Should have considered:** *Timothy*

Devon

GREG ALLMAN 😊

It means, we can reveal, 'from Devon'. That's something this Devon – son of the rock legend from Georgia – certainly is not.

> **Should have considered:** *Rutland*

Dex

True story: When the *Wayne's World* star and his wife were thinking of names they spotted a bottle of dextrose (sugar) on the table and simply shortened it. Dana himself was unfortunately named – his parents expected a girl and would not be shaken from the name they'd already picked.

Should have considered: *Caster*

Dexter

The name of the *Annie Hall* star's adopted daughter means 'right' in Latin, as opposed to 'left', rather than 'wrong'. SEE ALSO: *Duke*.

Should have considered: *Buster*

Dhani

The Beatle's son is named after two notes in the Indian scale, Dha and Ni. Lucky that George didn't use the Western scale.

Should have considered: *F-Sharp G*

Diezel

Inevitably Diezel will debate with brother Denim (see separate entry) as to who came off worst. Suffice to say the 'Unbreak My Heart' singer made a fuellish choice. SEE ALSO: *Denim*.

Should have considered: *Unledley*

Dilyn

Dillon means 'faithful'. But the *Baywatch* stunner couldn't remain faithful to the spelling – saddling her daughter with a lifetime of: 'You're spelling that how?'

Should have considered: *Dyll'un*

Diva Muffin

FRANK ZAPPA

The second in our list from the king of daft names. Diva means 'divine' and muffin means, well, a small cake. So this could mean 'fantastic cake'. But the reality is that eccentric rock genius Frank called her a diva (or prima donna) because she screamed louder than the other babies in the hospital. SEE ALSO: *Ahmet, Dweezil, Moon Unit*.

> **Should have considered:** *Blueberry Muffin*

Dixie Dot

ANNA RYDER RICHARDSON

Another alliterative name from the alliterative TV interior designer. Dixie is the nickname for the southern US states which rebelled against the Union. In French it means 'born tenth'. Luckily for Anna, Dixie's only the second. SEE ALSO: *Bibi Belle*.

> **Should have considered:** *Dulux Pot*

Django

DAVE STEWART & SIOBHAN FAHEY

The Eurythmics star and the Bananarama singer paid tribute to Django Reinhardt, the digitally challenged Belgian gipsy jazz guitar genius. SEE ALSO: *Kaya, Sam Hurricane*.

> **Should have considered:** *Ed Stewpot*

Domenica

MARTIN SCORSESE

An extra 'a' feminises Domenic for the director of *Goodfellas, Taxi Driver* and *Gangs of New York*.

> **Should have considered:** *Martina*

Domenick
STEVEN SEAGAL & KELLY LEBROCK 🙂

The B-movie actor and his model wife added a consonant to make their son stand out from the seething mass of standard Domenics. SEE ALSO: *Annaliza, Arrisa, Justice*.

Should have considered: *Jonathan Livingston*

Donte
PHIL SPECTOR 🙂

Presumably derived from the Italian Dante, meaning 'lasting', this was the name the legendary 1960s pop producer gave his adopted son.

Should have considered: *Ian*

Draven
CHESTER BENNINGTON 🙂

The frontman with hip-hop metallers Linkin' Park is a fan of gothic movie thriller *The Crow*. Draven is the lead character's surname. Little Draven can breathe a sigh of relief that removing just two letters will make him plain old Dave.

Should have considered: *Avenger*

Dream
GINUWINE 🙂

The daughter of the R 'n' B singer, real name Elgin Lumpkin, is guaranteed to grow up into a Dream girl. SEE ALSO: *Story*.

Should have considered: *Pumpkin*

Dree
MARIEL HEMINGWAY 🙂

Mariel, star of Woody Allen's *Manhattan* and granddaughter of Ernest Hemingway, was named after a Cuban fishing village. Her daughter's name means 'tedious' in old English. Hopefully Mariel was unaware of this. SEE ALSO: *Langley Fox*.

Should have considered: *Ernestine*

Duke

DIANE KEATON

The *Annie Hall* star handed her son a noble title when she adopted him in 2000. SEE ALSO: *Dexter*.

Should have considered: Earl

Dusti Rain

VANILLA ICE

Sorry Mr Ice, but what IS dusty rain? Doesn't rain damp down dust? Perhaps Ice, the white rapper Robert Matthew van Winkle, should tell us.

Should have considered: Rip

Dweezil

FRANK ZAPPA

'Dweezil' – from the Latin for 'guitar genius'. Just kidding. The real story is: rock star Frank wanted to call him Dweezil, short for 'Da weasel', a nickname he had for one of his wife's toes. But officials refused to register it and he was named Ian Donald Calvin Euclid Zappa. Eventually he changed his name to Dweezil. And became a guitar genius. SEE ALSO: *Ahmet, Diva Muffin, Moon Unit*.

Should have considered: DaStoat

Dylan Jagger

PAMELA ANDERSON & TOMMY LEE

The *Baywatch* star and the Motley Crüe drummer combined two of pop's greats. Note how the boy was not called Tommy.

Should have considered: Keef

Top 10 UK baby names

(From 2005)

boys

1. Jack
2. Joshua
3. Thomas
4. James
5. Oliver
6. Daniel
7. Samuel
8. William
9. Harry
10. Joseph

girls

1. Jessica
2. Emily
3. Sophie
4. Olivia
5. Chloe
6. Ellie
7. Grace
8. Lucy
9. Charlotte
10. Katie

Top 10 US baby names

(From 2004, latest figures available)

boys

1 Jacob
2 Michael
3 Joshua
4 Matthew
5 Ethan
6 Andrew
7 Daniel
8 William
9 Joseph
10 Christopher

girls

1 Emily
2 Emma
3 Madison
4 Olivia
5 Hannah
6 Abigail
7 Isabella
8 Ashley
9 Samantha
10 Elizabeth

Top 10 nutty celeb names

(selected by the author)

1   *Pilot Inspektor*

2   *Moxie CrimeFighter*

3   *Seven Sirius*

4   *Moon Unit*

5   *Speck Wildhorse*

6   *Jermajesty*

7   *Pirate*

8   *Oriole Nebula*

9   *Sage Moonblood*

10 *Whizdom*

E

FROM *Earvin* TO *Ezekiel*

Earvin
'MAGIC' JOHNSON ☺

This derives from Irvine, meaning 'lover of the sea', and is the LA Lakers basketball star's real first name. And his father's before him.

Should have considered: *Magic Jnr*

Eja
SHANIA TWAIN & ROBERT JOHN 'MUTT' LANGE ☺

Pronounced 'Asia', this oddity was the choice of the Canadian country singer, born Eilleen Regina Edwards, and her record producer husband. It Don't Impress Me Much.

Should have considered: *Africa*

Electra
DAVE MUSTAINE ☹

It means 'sparkling' in Greek but presumably the Megadeth thrash metaller's choice has more to do with conjuring up an image of high-voltage rock 'n' roll. Or something. SEE ALSO: *Justis*.

Should have considered: *Morticia*

Eliana
CHRISTIAN SLATER ☺

The *True Romance* star, who began life as Christian Michael Leonard Hawkins, picked a name meaning 'The Lord answers' in Hebrew.

Should have considered: *Seeya*

Elias Balthasar
BORIS BECKER & BARBARA FELTUS ☺

Elias is the Greek form of the Hebrew name Elijah, meaning 'God is Jehovah'. If the tennis legend's son ever wants to change it, Elias will need an alias.

Should have considered: *Decker*

Elijah Blue
CHER & GREG ALLMAN

Colourful mix of traditional and modern for the son of Cher and rocker Greg Allman. I Got Blue Babe!

Should have considered: Blacken Blue

Elijah Patricius Bob Guggi Q
BONO

The U2 frontman, real name Paul David Hewson, paid tribute to an old mate, nicknamed Guggi. Bob is variously said to be for Bono's dad or Bob Dylan. Q? A rock magazine? James Bond's gadget maker? SEE ALSO: *Memphis*.

Should have considered: M

Elisha
MICHAEL ANTHONY

Van Halen's bass player picked a traditionally male Hebrew name meaning 'God is salvation'.

Should have considered: Marque

Ella Bleu
JOHN TRAVOLTA & KELLY PRESTON

Bleu? Pourquoi? Maybe it's a reminder of the wild bleu yonder the *Pulp Fiction* star flies around in his Boeing. SEE ALSO: *Jett*.

Should have considered: Qantas

Ellery
LAURA DERN & BEN HARPER

The name means 'lives by the alder tree' – but did the *Jurassic Park* actress and the blues musician name their son after the fictional detective Ellery Queen? It's a mystery.

Should have considered: Sherlock

Elroy

NEIL FINN

The gifted Crowded House singer chose a name deriving from Leroy, a French name meaning 'King'.

Should have considered: *Mickey*

Elvis

ROMAN POLANSKI & EMMANUELLE SEIGNER

No prizes for guessing the film director's inspiration here. Elvis is an Anglo-Saxon name for 'wise' – like Polanski's decision not to return to the States.

Should have considered: *King*

Emerson

TERI HATCHER

Lovely, lovely, lovely. And that's just Teri. If the Desperate Housewife wants to name her daughter after the keyboard player from Emerson, Lake and Palmer, we'll stand up, salute and hum 'Fanfare for the Common Man'.

Should have considered: *Margaret*

Esme

ANTHONY EDWARDS

Means 'kind defender' in Anglo-Saxon – not a bad description of Anthony as Dr Mark Greene on *ER*. SEE ALSO: *Bailey, Wallis*.

Should have considered: *Blake*

Eugenie

PRINCE ANDREW & SARAH FERGUSON

It comes from the French for 'well-born', which indeed the little Windsor was.

Should have considered: *Barbara*

Eulala

MARCIA GAY HARDEN

Ooh la la! This lass seems to have been named after a random burst of singsong by the star of *Miller's Crossing* and *Mystic River*. SEE ALSO: *Hudson, Julitta Dee*.

Should have considered: *Tumteetumtum*

Evie

SEAN BEAN

A diminutive of the Biblical name Eve, meaning 'life'. She, you will recall, starred in the Book of Genesis. Sean starred in another blockbuster, *Lord of the Rings*.

Should have considered: *Jean*

Ezekiel

BEAU BRIDGES

A most apt name, this – Ezekiel being the Old Testament prophet who loved drama and songwriting. Beau is a movie actor who loves playing guitar.

Should have considered: *Bernie*

F

FROM *Fifi* TO *Fuschia*

Fifi Trixibelle
BOB GELDOF & PAULA YATES

There are those who would say this is suitable only for a small yapping dog. We wouldn't be among them. Anything Saint Bob does or says is OK by us. SEE ALSO: *Peaches Honeyblossom, Pixie, Heavenly Hiraani Tiger Lily*.

Should have considered: *Does not apply*

Finlay
SADIE FROST & GARY KEMP

The actress and the Spandau Ballet guitarist had a 'small blond soldier'. That's its original meaning, anyway.

Should have considered: *Ross*

Fire
STEVE VAI

Imagine the rumpus when dad, the guitar virtuoso, calls his lad in for tea: 'Fire! Fire!' 999 crews will be there every evening.

Should have considered: *The neighbours*

Frankito
TRE COOL

Green Day's drummer was born Frank Edwin Wright III. His son's name apparently means 'Little Frank'. SEE ALSO: *Ramona*.

Should have considered: *Orville*

Free
DAVID CARRADINE & BARBARA HERSHEY

He was great in *Kill Bill 2*. She was great in *Hannah and Her Sisters*. In the early 1970s they were the epitome of the hippy couple, having a son called Free. What Free did next is elsewhere in the book (see 'You've got to be kidding', page 133). But here's a footnote about his mum: Around 1972 she ran over a seagull and felt its spirit enter her. Already an established actress, she spent two years known as Barbara Seagull. SEE ALSO: *Calista, Kansas*.

Should have considered: *Marrying Steven Seagal*

Freedom
VING RHAMES

This means much to the man who was Marcellus Wallace in *Pulp Fiction* and is now Kojak. 'I gave him that name because he is the first male child of the Rhames family not born into poverty,' he says. SEE ALSO: *Reignbeau*.

Should have considered: *Bling*

Freya
ADRIAN EDMONDSON & JENNIFER SAUNDERS

In Anglo-Saxon it means 'Queen of the Gods'. Which sounds like a heavy metal number TV comic Ade's band Bad News might have written.

Should have considered: *Vyvyan*

Fuddy
DAMON WAYANS

Oddly enough this has no meaning in ancient Anglo-Saxon. No meaning in any language, in fact. It seems particularly daft to us, but maybe we are fuddy-duddies.

Should have considered: *John*

Fuschia
STING

Who knows why the great singer/songwriter Gordon Sumner picked this one? Maybe his daughter was a purplish red when she emerged into the world. SEE ALSO: *Giacomo*.

Should have considered: *Summer*

G

FROM *Gabriel* TO *Gunner*

Gabriel Luke Beauregard

MICK JAGGER & JERRY HALL

Funnily enough, the Archangel Gabriel appeared in the Book of Luke. As for Beauregard, he can thank Jerry's Texan roots – Beauregard being a Confederate General during the Civil War.

Should have considered: Lee

Gabriel-Kane

DANIEL DAY-LEWIS

The Irish star of *Gangs of New York* must reckon his lad is an angel. SEE ALSO: *Cashel Blake*.

Should have considered: Seraphim

Gabriel Wilk

MIA FARROW

A wilk is a variation of 'whelk', the popular sea creature. However, Gabriel was named after Judge Wilk, who ruled in Mia's favour in her custody battle with Woody Allen. See entry on page 173 for a full list of Mia Farrow's children.

Should have considered: No hard feelings

Gaia

EMMA THOMPSON

Gaia is a planet in *Star Trek*. It is also a firm of Frisbee-makers and the initials of the Grantley Adams International Airport in Barbados. But we suspect its original meaning – 'Mother Earth' in Greek and Roman mythology – drew the movie actress to it.

Should have considered: Vulcan

Galen Grier

DENNIS HOPPER

The *Easy Rider* star chose a Gaelic name meaning 'tranquil' – which sums up his life. Not!

Should have considered: Grass

Gene

LIAM GALLAGHER & NICOLE APPLETON

OK, as Tom Jones would say, it's not unusual. Nonetheless the choice of the Oasis frontman and the All Saints singer is worth recording because of the poetic motive behind it. As Nic explained: 'You can't f*** around with Gene. You can't turn it into a silly nickname.'

Should have considered: *Geno, Genius, Gene Genie, Genoa, the Genester*

George

GEORGE FOREMAN

Not an unusual name at all, especially in the home of George Foreman. The heavyweight boxing legend and low-fat grillmeister's inclusion in this book is simply to record the SEVEN kids named after him. This one's his first son.

Should have considered: *Audio Science*

George Jnr

GEORGE FOREMAN

This is another George.

Should have considered: *Dweezil*

George III

GEORGE FOREMAN

So is this.

Should have considered: *Pilot Inspektor*

George IV

GEORGE FOREMAN

This is another one.

Should have considered: *Fire*

George V

GEORGE FOREMAN

And another.

> *Should have considered:* Hendrix Halen

George VI

GEORGE FOREMAN

That's the last of his sons.

> *Should have considered:* Seven Sirius

Georgetta

GEORGE FOREMAN

This is his daughter.

> *Should have considered:* Fifi Trixibelle

Geronimo

ALEX JAMES

Blur's bass player presumably hopes his little lad will have some of the Apache's fighting spirit. He'll probably be a librarian.

> *Should have considered:* Jesse

Giacomo

STING

Gordon Sumner's boy has a lovely Italian name meaning 'supplanter' – 'one who replaces'. A racehorse named after him won the Kentucky Derby at 50-1. The owner was Sting's mate. SEE ALSO: *Fuschia*.

> *Should have considered:* Arkle

Greer

KELSEY GRAMMER

The *Cheers* and *Frasier* star picked a Scottish name meaning 'alert'. Unfortunately the 'Gr, Gr' alliteration makes it sound like it was made up by Tony, the Frosties tiger. SEE ALSO: *Mason*.

> *Should have considered:* Grrreek

Greta
KEVIN KLINE & PHOEBE CATES

A Swedish form of Margaret, most famously the first name of movie star Greta Garbo. Which is apt considering her movie star parents.

> ***Should have considered:*** *Patsy*

Griffin
BRENDAN FRASER

The film star chose a Welsh name meaning 'strong in faith'. Presumably Brendan has already cracked the 'Mummy Returns' gag when the missus gets back from the shops.

> ***Should have considered:*** *Mad Frankie*

Gulliver
GARY OLDMAN

Top name, from the 1726 Jonathan Swift novel *Gulliver's Travels*, but why the *Dracula* and *Harry Potter* star picked it is a mystery. Perhaps his lad was much bigger than the others in the maternity unit.

> ***Should have considered:*** *Grumpy*

Gunner
NIKKI SIXX

More 'double consonant' action from the Motley Crüe bassist. If he uses dad's stage name he'll have to sign official forms as Sixx, Gunner. SEE ALSO: *Dekker, Storm Brieanne*.

> ***Should have considered:*** *Hitfer*

FROM *Hailie* TO *Hudson*

Hailie

EMINEM & KIM MATHERS ☺

The Oscar and Grammy-winning rap icon, real name Marshall Bruce Mathers III, took an ordinary girl's name and gave the spelling a tweak.

Should have considered: Martha Fokker

Hana Aluna

KENNY LOGGINS ☺

The Footloose singer apparently fell in love with the unspoiled Hawaiian town of Hana.

Should have considered: Aloha

Happy

MACY GRAY ☺

Well, the R 'n' B singer needed something cheerful to balance that grey surname. Happy is a lot to live up to, though.

Should have considered: Reasonably content

Harlow

PATRICIA ARQUETTE ☺

Its actual meaning is 'from the hare's hill'. It is remotely possible the *True Romance* star was paying tribute to the Essex new town (population 80,000), but it is more likely to refer to Jean Harlow, the movies' 'original blonde bombshell' of the 1920s. Especially with Patricia being a blonde bombshell of the 1990s.

Should have considered: Monroe

Harrison

JAMES MAJOR & EMMA NOBLE ☺

A rare enough name until Harrison Ford became a star. And John Major's son and his model ex have shortened it to Harry.

Should have considered: Sergeant

Harvey Kirby
JONATHAN ROSS & JANE GOLDMAN

Harvey is ordinary enough. Kirby is for one of the TV host's heroes, Jack Kirby, a cartoonist who created the Hulk. SEE ALSO: *Betty Kitten, Honey Kinney.*

Should have considered: *Charlie Farley*

Healey
DREW BLEDSOE

Doubtless Lord Healey, once Labour Chancellor, would be chuffed to bits at this tribute from a most unlikely source. Unfortunately the Dallas Cowboys quarterback had something else in mind. We know not what.

Should have considered: *Kinnock*

Heaven
L'IL MO

Whether the R 'n' B singer, real name Cynthia Loving, still thinks of her daughter as Heaven when she's red in the face, throwing a tantrum and refusing to eat her tea is questionable.

Should have considered: *Hereafter*

Heavenly Hiraani Tiger Lily
PAULA YATES & MICHAEL HUTCHENCE

Paula's daughters with Bob Geldof (Fifi Trixibelle, Peaches and Pixie) are said to have picked Heavenly and Tiger Lily (after the Peter Pan character). Hiraani was the choice of the INXS singer, as it's Polynesian for 'Princess of the Sky'. So, you see … it makes perfect sense. She's now known simply as Tiger.

Should have considered: *Not asking the kids*

Hendrix Halen Michael Rhoads
ZAKK WYLDE (icon)

Guitar tributes galore by the Ozzy Osbourne axeman: Jimi Hendrix; Eddie Van Halen; Randy Rhoads and Michael ... er ... Schenker? Or is Michael for the boy's godfather, New York Mets baseball legend Mike Piazza? Zakk himself is worried about the boy's name: 'I know he's going to be into basket-weaving and crochet or ballet, or he's going to be a Chippendale's dancer. I can see it comin'.'

Should have considered: *Oscar*

Holden
BRENDAN FRASER (icon)

The meaning is 'from the hollow in the valley' – and the inspiration likely to be Holden Caulfield, teenage hero of the classic novel *The Catcher in the Rye*.

Should have considered: *Vernon God*

Hollee
THE EDGE (icon)

Despite the gimmicky spelling, this is possibly the most 'normal' name among the U2 guitarist's children. SEE ALSO: *Arun, Blue Angel, Levi.*

Should have considered: *Holly*

Homer
RICHARD GERE (icon)

D'oh! What was the *Pretty Woman* star thinking? It's like *The Simpsons* never happened.

Should have considered: *Gottla*

Honey Kinney

JONATHAN ROSS & JANE GOLDMAN

Sorry Jonathan ... Britain will never elect a Prime Minister called Honey. Kinney was apparently in honour of Jane's childhood nanny. SEE ALSO: *Betty Kitten, Harvey Kirby*.

Should have considered: *Diana*

Hopper Jack

SEAN PENN & ROBIN WRIGHT PENN

The *Mystic River* Oscar-winner, honoured two movie mavericks who inspired him and became his friends, Dennis Hopper and Jack Nicholson.

Should have considered: *Brando Clint*

Hud

JOHN MELLENCAMP

The 'Jack and Diane' singer, once John 'Cougar' Mellencamp, paid tribute to Paul Newman's cool movie cowboy. Let's hope the boy won't develop Hud's drinking habits. SEE ALSO: *Speck Wildhorse*.

Should have considered: *Cat Ballou*

Hudson

MARCIA GAY HARDEN

It means 'son of the hooded man', which is all very sinister. But maybe *Mystic River* star Marcia has a thing about rivers. SEE ALSO: *Eulala, Julitta Dee*.

Should have considered: *Mystic*

Baby place

Kids named after cities, countries, landmarks etc.

Aquinnah	MICHAEL J FOX & TRACY POLLAN ☺
Assisi	JADE JAGGER ☺
Atlanta Noo	JOHN TAYLOR & AMANDA DE CADENET ☺
Avalon	MIKE KROEGER ☺
Boston	KURT RUSSELL ☺
Brooklyn	DAVID & VICTORIA BECKHAM ☺
Bryce Dallas	RON HOWARD ☺
China	GRACE SLICK ☺
Chynna	MICHELLE PHILLIPS ☺
Dakota Mayi	DON JOHNSON & MELANIE GRIFFITH ☺
Deni Montana	WOODY HARRELSON ☺
Devon	GREG ALLMAN ☺
Gaia	EMMA THOMPSON ☺
Hana Aluna	KENNY LOGGINS ☺
Harlow	PATRICIA ARQUETTE ☺
Indiana August	CASEY AFFLECK & SUMMER PHOENIX ☺
Ione Skye	DONOVAN ☺
Ireland	KIM BASINGER & ALEC BALDWIN ☺
Italia	LL COOL J ☺
Jasper Breckenridge	DON JOHNSON ☺
Jersey	NICKY BUTT ☺

Jorja	BRET MICHAELS
Kansas	DAVID CARRADINE
Karolina	STACY KEACH
Kenya	QUINCY JONES & NASTASSJA KINSKI
Langley Fox	MARIEL HEMINGWAY
London Emilio	SLASH
London Siddartha Halford	SEBASTIAN BACH
Lourdes Maria	MADONNA
Madison	ROBBIE FOWLER
Makena'lei	HELEN HUNT
Memphis	BONO
Montana	RICHARD THOMAS
Moon Unit	FRANK ZAPPA
Navarone	PRISCILLA PRESLEY
Paris Michael	MICHAEL JACKSON & DEBBIE ROWE
Persia	GARY NUMAN
Saffron Sahara	SIMON & YASMIN LE BON
Samaria	LL COOL J
Sean Preston	BRITNEY SPEARS & KEVIN FEDERLINE
Zion	LAURYN HILL

FROM *Indiana* TO *Italia*

Indiana August   CASEY AFFLECK & SUMMER PHOENIX

Phoenix in the summer, Indiana in August. Sounds like a busy schedule for Casey, of *Ocean's Eleven* and *Twelve* fame, and Summer, sister of River and Joaquin (formerly Leaf).

Should have considered: *Paris Spring*

Indio   ROBERT DOWNEY JR

Cool name from the brilliant Chaplin star – though its meaning is unclear.

Should have considered: *Eidur*

Ione Skye   DONOVAN

The Scottish folk singer, Donovan Philips Leitch, chose Ione, meaning 'from the king's island' and the island itself, Skye. It's said his daughter was conceived there. SEE ALSO: *Astrella Celeste, Oriole Nebula*.

Should have considered: *Isla Lewis*

Ireland   KIM BASINGER & ALEC BALDWIN

You have to really love a country to name your child after it – but the *LA Confidential* actress (real name Kimila Ann Basinger) and her movie star ex did just that.

Should have considered: *United Kingdom of Great Britain and Northern Ireland*

Iris   SADIE FROST & JUDE LAW

Iris was a messenger from the Gods in Greek myth. It is also a plant, of course. And the first name of the great author Iris Murdoch. SEE ALSO: *Rafferty*.

Should have considered: *Chrysanthemum*

Isadora

BJÖRK

The quirky Icelandic singer's tribute, we assume, to Isadora Duncan, the American dancer of the early 1900s who was strangled by her scarf. SEE ALSO: *Sindri*.

> **Should have considered:** *Ginger*

Iset

WESLEY SNIPES

So it's Iset, is it not? It is Iset? I see! What was the *New Jack City* star thinking with this baffling little concoction? Was he aiming for Ice T?

> **Should have considered:** *iPod*

Italia

LL COOL J

The hip-hop star, real name James Todd Smith (his stage name stands for 'Ladies Love Cool James'), should get together with Kim Basinger so Ireland and Italia can meet. We fancy Italia to win on penalties. SEE ALSO: *Najee, Samaria*.

> **Should have considered:** *Espana*

J

FROM *Jade* TO *Justis*

Jade Sheena Jezebel   MICK & BIANCA JAGGER 👶

Jade is, of course, a semi-precious stone – and aptly enough she now designs jewellery. Jezebel, long synonymous with 'wicked woman', is an odd one for a baby girl. And as Ramones fans will know, Sheena Is A Punk Rocker.

Should have considered: Vixen

Jaden Christopher Syre   WILL SMITH & JADA PINKETT SMITH 👶

The *Men in Black* star may be keen on fancy first names to balance his common-or-garden surname. Actress wife Jada was presumably the inspiration for Jaden. SEE ALSO: *Willard, Willow*.

Should have considered: Mel

Jaden Gil   ANDRE AGASSI & STEFFI GRAF 👶

Jaden means 'God has heard' in Hebrew. Where the tennis superstars found Gil is a mystery. SEE ALSO: *Jaz Elle*.

Should have considered: Sampras

Jagger   SCOTT STAPP 👶

Little doubt as to the inspiration for the controversial singer with heavy rock outfit Creed. We fear Jagger Stapp will get no satisfaction from it.

Should have considered: Keef

Jakob   BOB DYLAN 👶

The Biblical name Jacob means 'supplanter'. Was the great singer/songwriter/poet encouraging his son to usurp him? Not sure his band The Wallflowers has quite done that.

Should have considered: Matt

Jakob Danger   BILLIE JOE ARMSTRONG ☺

The frontman with neo-punks Green Day is trying a tad hard – adding a 'dangerous' K to Jacob and then, as if we don't get it, actually calling the poor boy Danger! Kids and danger shouldn't mix.

Should have considered: Lance, Neil

Jameson Ivor   JONATHAN FRAKES ☺

Riker on *Star Trek, The Next Generation* named his son after both the lad's grandfathers, James and Ivor. Jameson is the first of Jonathan's next generation.

Should have considered: Picard

Jameson Leon   BILLY BALDWIN & CHYNNA PHILLIPS ☺

Jameson means son of James. And Leon's from the male name Leo, so it's a strange choice for the daughter of the *Backdraft* star and his ex-pop singer wife. SEE ALSO: *Vance*.

Should have considered: Stanley

Jamison   JIM BELUSHI ☺

The less talented brother of *Saturday Night Live* genius John picked a modern female derivation of his own name, James. SEE ALSO: *Jared*.

Should have considered: Hulla

Jared   JIM BELUSHI ☺

One place further on alphabetically is Jim's second unusually-named child. This one's a Hebrew name meaning 'he descends', though its popularity is ascending. SEE ALSO: *Jamison*.

Should have considered: Belisha

Jasper Breckenridge

DON JOHNSON

Jasper? OK Don, we're with you so far. But Breckenridge? We guess it's for the top Colorado ski resort. The *Miami Vice* and *Nash Bridges* star is a keen skier and got married in Aspen. SEE ALSO: *Atherton Grace*.

Should have considered: Buttermilk Telluride

Jaya

R KELLY

The R 'n' B giant, who sang 'I Believe I Can Fly' and whose real name is Robert Sylvester Kelly, chose a Hindi name meaning 'victory'. Well, he is a winner.

Should have considered: Kelly

Jaz Elle

ANDRE AGASSI & STEFFI GRAF

The tennis aces served up a seriously barmy name for their daughter. Perhaps she has great rhythm. SEE ALSO: *Jaden Gil*.

Should have considered: Bebop

Jazz Domino

JOE STRUMMER

The Clash icon, real name John Graham Mellor, loved jazz. And a clue to the second name may lie in the fact he covered a Fats Domino song on the album released after his death. SEE ALSO: *Lola Maybellene*.

Should have considered: Fats

Jenna

DUSTIN HOFFMAN

Short form of Jennifer, meaning 'white and smooth', which perhaps the *Rain Man* star's daughter is.

Should have considered: Tootsie

Jermajesty
JERMAINE JACKSON 😊

What jermean, Jermaine? Jergot to reconsider! Michael Jackson's brother took leave of his senses when he stuck this royal title on his son. As if he didn't have enough trouble being born into the Jackson clan. SEE ALSO: *Jourdyn*.

Should have considered: *Jeravinalaugh*

Jersey
NICKY BUTT 😊

Did the Newcastle and ex-Manchester United player ape his mate David Beckham and name his daughter after where she was conceived? He's not telling. If he has another child he should call it exactly the same name. Then he'll have a replica Jersey.

Should have considered: *Slapmy*

Jessamine
PAUL WELLER 😊

The Jam and Style Council frontman picked a variation of Jasmine (after the plant).

Should have considered: *Bella*

Jesse James
JON BON JOVI 😊

The rock singer, born Giovanni Bongiovanni, has a thing about the Wild West, which explains this tribute to the Missouri outlaw.

Should have considered: *Billy Bonney*

Jett
JOHN TRAVOLTA & KELLY PRESTON 😊

No prizes for figuring this one out. The *Pulp Fiction* star is a qualified pilot who owns five planes, including a former Qantas Airlines Boeing 707 with Jett emblazoned on its side. SEE ALSO: *Ella Bleu*.

Should have considered: *Airbus*

Jonas
JAMIE FARR

He may have been bonkers in *M*A*S*H* as Corporal Klinger, but Jamie Farr's choice is a known derivation of Jonah, a Biblical name meaning 'dove'.

Should have considered: Run

Jones
CERYS MATTHEWS

The Catatonia star named her son after fellow Welsh singer Tom Jones, whose gig she was en route to when she went into labour. Thank heavens she wasn't going to see Babyshambles.

Should have considered: Shakey

Jorja
BRET MICHAELS

Georgia, nice name. But Jorja? The singer with rock band Poison saddled his daughter with a lifetime of spelling out her name.

Should have considered: Phlawda

Jourdyn
JERMAINE JACKSON

Has Jermaine taken spelling lessons from Bret Michaels? What's wrong with plain Jordan? It could have been worse, though, Jordy. Just ask your brother Jermajesty (see separate entry).

Should have considered: Jordan

Jude
MACKENZIE CROOK

A form of Judah, meaning 'he who is praised' – as his dad was for playing pedantic Gareth in *The Office*.

Should have considered: Total

Julitta Dee   MARCIA GAY HARDEN

The *Miller's Crossing* star's daughter is a little Saint – St Julitta died in the 4th century. SEE ALSO: *Eulala, Hudson*.

Should have considered: *Juletta F*

Junior Savva   KATIE 'JORDAN' PRICE & PETER ANDRE

The ex-Page 3 girl says Junior is a way of saying he's a 'mini-Pete'. Savva is after pop star Pete's Greek dad. Junior Savva is unusual but, as Jordan says: 'At least it's not Apples and Pears or whatever.'

Should have considered: *Gwyneth's feelings*

Justice   STEVEN SEAGAL

A strong, noble word, but it's not a boy's name, is it Steve? And how he must have worried when you made the movie *Out for Justice*. SEE ALSO: *Annaliza, Arrisa, Domenick*.

Should have considered: *Vengeance*

Justis   DAVE MUSTAINE

Right, thought the Megadeth star, calling him Justice isn't enough. What else can I do? SEE ALSO: *Electra*.

Should have considered: *Juzztizz*

K

FROM *Kahlea* TO *Kyla*

Kahlea

DANIEL BALDWIN

Continuing a theme of baffling spellings, one of Alec Baldwin's actor brothers gives us Carly, as Kahlea.

Should have considered: *Karli*

Kai

JENNIFER CONNELLY

Kai has different meanings in different languages. The *Beautiful Mind* star may have chosen it as Hawaiian for 'the sea' or Navajo for 'willow tree'.

Should have considered: *Billy*

Kaia Jordan

CINDY CRAWFORD & RANDE GERBER

Kaia is a female variation of Kai (see above). And Jordan … a tribute from one model to another? Unlikely. SEE ALSO: *Presley*.

Should have considered: *Jabba*

Kaiis

GEENA DAVIS

Kai is what? This is the *Thelma and Louise* star's twin son. SEE ALSO: *Kian*.

Should have considered: *Kaioona*

Kailand

STEVIE WONDER

Kailand? Land of the Kais? Or presumably 'land of the sea' in Hawaiian. In fact this is a mix of the Motown legend's real name Steveland Morris and his wife's name Kai. SEE ALSO: *Mandla Kadjay Carl*.

Should have considered: *Wonderland*

Kal-El

NICOLAS CAGE

This isn't from Hawaii, in case you wondered. It's from Krypton. Kal-El was Superman's name before he arrived on Earth and became Clark Kent. And unless the *Leaving Las Vegas* star's son develops X-ray vision or incredible strength, he'll never live up to it. SEE ALSO: *Weston*.

Should have considered: *Bruce Wayne*

Kaleb

KEVIN FEDERLINE

In Hebrew it means 'bold', which his dad certainly was, leaving his ex and marrying Britney Spears two months after Kaleb was born.

Should have considered: *Fred*

Kama

SAMMY HAGAR

The ex-Van Halen singer and solo artist picked a word which in Hindi means 'love'. Well, Why Can't This Be Love?

Should have considered: *Horrible*

Kansas

DAVID CARRADINE

What is the *Kill Bill* star implying? That his daughter's a state? SEE ALSO: *Calista, Free*.

Should have considered: *Nebraska*

Karis

MICK JAGGER & MARSHA HUNT

The Rolling Stone fathered Karis with the star of hippy musical *Hair*. It's a Greek name meaning 'grace'.

Should have considered: *Michaela*

Karolina

STACY KEACH

The star who played TV detective Mike Hammer was born in Georgia, next to the Carolinas. Who knows if that inspired him? The 'K' was all a bit unnecessary.

Should have considered: *Kalifornia*

Karsen

RAY LIOTTA

An unusual form of Carson, meaning 'son of Carr'. She's a girl, but who's arguing with the *Goodfellas* star? This is a bloke who comes round if you spill your Heineken.

Should have considered: *Whatever Ray wants is fine*

Kathryne

TYNE DALY

Another tricksy vowel change from the *Cagney and Lacey* star. Katherine means 'pure', by the way. SEE ALSO: *Alisabeth, Alyxandra.*

Should have considered: *Kithryn*

Katia

DENZEL WASHINGTON

The *Philadelphia* and *Training Day* star picked the Slavic derivation of Kate, short for Katherine.

Should have considered: *Georgia*

Kaya

DAVE STEWART & SIOBHAN FAHEY

Who's That Girl? Well, she's the youngest of the Eurythmics star's three kids, which is odd because her name is Hopi Indian for 'elder sister'. SEE ALSO: *Django, Sam Hurricane.*

Should have considered: *Moira*

Kecalf

Did the soul singer give birth at the start of a soccer match? We can think of no other explanation.

Should have considered: *Haftime*

Keegan

Tempting though it is to speculate that the skateboard genius named his son after Kevin Keegan, the name simply means 'small and fiery' in Gaelic. Just like Kevin.

Should have considered: *Keano*

Kenya

The movie composer/record producer and his actress girlfriend named their daughter after the East African country (population 32 million).

Should have considered: *Sudan*

Kian

The *Thelma and Louise* star's twin son. In mischievous moods he and brother Kaiis could swap their vowels. Mum would never know. SEE ALSO: *Kaiis*.

Should have considered: *Kanis, Kain, Iakis*

Kiki

A very showbizzy name from evil Janine Butcher in *EastEnders*. Kiki was the stage name of actress, model and painter Alice Prin in the 1920s, as well as the first name of singer/songwriter Kiki Dee. Kiki was also the frog in the kids' show *Hector's House*.

Should have considered: *Elkie*

Kit

JODIE FOSTER

The double Oscar-winning *Silence of the Lambs* actress, real name Alicia Christian Foster, gave her second son a diminutive of Christopher. He was not named in honour of the pregnancy test.

Should have considered: *Brendan*

Kitt

EARTHA KITT

The singing legend was keen to pass on something of her name to her daughter – and although this choice raised the wonderful prospect of Kitt Kitt, she is actually known as Kitt Shapiro. Namesakes include the talking car in *Knight Rider*.

Should have considered: *Football*

Kyd

DAVID DUCHOVNY & TEA LEONI

A kid called Kyd? How long did that take them? You'd think with *X Files* and *Deep Impact* between them there would have been a host of sci-fi possibilities.

Should have considered: *Hal*

Kyla Avril

GEDDY LEE

The Canadian-Jewish singer and virtuoso bassist with rock giants Rush picked a Hebrew word for 'victory'. Aptly enough their 2002 album opened with 'One Little Victory' and ended with 'Out of the Cradle'. Which may have nothing to do with anything.

Should have considered: *Peggy*

L

FROM *Laird* TO *Lux*

Laird Vonne

SHARON STONE

The *Basic Instinct* star's middle name is Vonne, so she gave it to her adopted son, too. Laird is, of course, Scottish for 'lord'. Pity the poor laird. SEE ALSO: *Roan*.

Should have considered: Rolan

Landon

BOBBY BROWN

The R 'n' B singer picked an old English word meaning 'from the long hill'. Hey, it's his prerogative. SEE ALSO: *Laprincia*.

Should have considered: Roy Chubby

Langley Fox

MARIEL HEMINGWAY

It's tempting to speculate that the *Manhattan* movie star named her daughter after a fox she ran over on the M4 near Slough (stranger things have happened – see entry for Free), but it's probably not so. Langley means 'from the long meadow'. Fox means 'fox'. SEE ALSO: *Dree*.

Should have considered: Bracknell Bunny

Langston

LAURENCE FISHBURNE

Authorities vary on what Langston means – either 'from the long enclosure' or 'town of the giant'. Well, *Matrix* fans, perhaps it depends whether you take the blue pill or the red.

Should have considered: Morpheus

Laprincia

BOBBY BROWN

The R 'n' B singer stuck his daughter with a truly awful invention. A bit rich coming from the man with an album titled *Don't Be Cruel*. SEE ALSO: *Landon*.

Should have considered: Jackie

Lark Song

MIA FARROW

Lark song is very nice, of course, Mia ... but not as a name. See 'Mamma Mia', page 173, for a list of all Mia Farrow's children.

Should have considered: *Tweetie*

Layne

LARS ULRICH

Seems to be a road movie theme going on with the Metallica drummer. First son was Myles, second is Layne. Is that fast layne or slow layne?

Should have considered: *Central Reservaytion*

Leni

HEIDI KLUM & FLAVIO BRIATORE

The German supermodel and her ex, the Italian race-car tycoon, took the name of Heidi's gran. It derives from Helena, itself from Helen, Greek for 'bright one'.

Should have considered: *Bree*

Lennon

LIAM GALLAGHER & PATSY KENSIT

The Oasis singer and his actress ex-wife chose Liam's hero and inspiration John Lennon. Some Might Say it was cruel on the lad but Liam decided to Roll With It.

Should have considered: *Macca*

Levi

THE EDGE

The U2 guitarist Dave Evans has delved into his handy Bible and plucked out the Hebrew name for 'united'. SEE ALSO: *Arun, Blue Angel, Hollee*.

Should have considered: *Moses*

Levon Roan
UMA THURMAN & ETHAN HAWKE

Cool name, meaning unclear. Famous Levons include Levon Helm, drummer with The Band and, er, that's it. Backwards, it spells novel, two of which Ethan has written. OK, we're clutching at straws. SEE ALSO: *Maya*.

Should have considered: *Sparrow*

Liberty
RYAN GIGGS

The Manchester United winger's daughter was born the day Saddam Hussein's regime was toppled. The *Sun*'s headline said 'STATUE OF LIBERTY' as monuments to him fell. Poetic, eh?

Should have considered: *Frieda*

Lightfield
GEOFFREY LEWIS

No clues to what inspired this – and Lewis opted for the more conventional Juliette for his actress daughter. Among the many Clint Eastwood movies he appeared in was *Thunderbolt and Lightfoot*. Which is a bit like Lightfield. We did say 'a bit'.

Should have considered: *Lightsaber*

Lila Grace
KATE MOSS & JEFFERSON HACK

Derivation of Lily, and vaguely interesting because that's what her ex Johnny Depp called his baby three years before Kate's.

Should have considered: *Jacqui*

Lily-Rose Melody
JOHNNY DEPP & VANESSA PARADIS

Double flower action for the *Pirates of the Caribbean* star's daughter. Presumably Melody is for her mum, the French 'Joe Le Taxi' singer.

Should have considered: *Bluebell-Buttercup*

Lilyella
MELANIE BLATT

Can't choose between Lily and Ella? Follow the All Saint and have both!

Should have considered: Lily, Ella

Loewy
JOHN MALKOVICH

The star of *In the Line of Fire* and *Dangerous Liaisons* is a fan of the great American industrial designer Raymond Loewy, who created planes, trains, automobiles and fridges. SEE ALSO: *Amandine*.

Should have considered: Dyson

Logan Romero
ROBERT PLANT

The first name the Led Zeppelin star picked means 'from the little hollow'. The second is anyone's guess. SEE ALSO: *Carmen*.

Should have considered: Pot

Lola
SARA COX & JON CARTER

Short form of the French name Dolores, meaning 'sorrow', which is not very uplifting for the wee lass. It's also a transvestite in a Kinks song. Nice name, though.

Should have considered: Lilo

Lola Maybellene
JOE STRUMMER

The terrific second name derives from Mabel, meaning 'lovable', and must be connected to Chuck Berry's first single, the classic 'Maybellene'. SEE ALSO: *Jazz Domino*.

Should have considered: Joni B Goode

Lola Simone

CHRIS ROCK

The comedian who occasionally hosts the Oscars apparently admitted that in hindsight his daughter's name would not look out of place on a pole-dancer. You said it, Chris. SEE ALSO: *Zahra Savannah*.

Should have considered: *Brandi Foxx*

London Emilio

SLASH

The ex-Guns 'n' Roses guitarist, real name Saul Hudson, conceived his son in London. Meanwhile Emilio is Spanish for 'flatterer'. SEE ALSO: *Cash*.

Should have considered: *Stoke*

London Siddartha Halford

SEBASTIAN BACH

Another heavy rocker picks London. This time it's Skid Row's singer, who also opted for Siddartha, Buddha's original name, and Halford – either a tribute to gay Judas Priest singer Rob Halford or the popular car accessories shop.

Should have considered: *Johann*

Lorca

LEONARD COHEN

Murdered Spanish poet Federico Garcia Lorca heavily influenced the veteran singer/songwriter.

Should have considered: *Betjeman*

Lorenzo Aureolino

NUNO BETTENCOURT

The former Extreme guitar genius went with the Spanish form of Laurence, followed by what seems to be a derivation of the word aureole, meaning halo. SEE ALSO: *Bebe Orleans*.

Should have considered: *Borealis*

Lourdes Maria

MADONNA

The superstar, full name Madonna Louise Ciccone, was raised a Catholic and enraged the Church by naming her daughter after the holy site in the South of France. SEE ALSO: *Rocco*.

Should have considered: *Fatima*

Luca

COLIN FIRTH & LIVIA GIUGGIOLI

Perhaps best known as Mr Darcy in TV's *Pride and Prejudice*, the movie star is married to Italian film producer Livia Giuggioli, hence his sons' Italian names. This means 'bringer of light'. SEE ALSO: *Mateo*.

Should have considered: *Santino*

Lucian

STEVE BUSCEMI

This choice, from the *Reservoir Dogs* and *Fargo* star, means 'man of light'.

Should have considered: *Pink*

Lulu

PAUL SIMON & EDIE BRICKELL

No idea why they picked the short form of Louise, unless the music legend and his singing wife are secret fans of our very own Lulu (Marie McDonald McLaughlin Lawrie).

Should have considered: *Carly*

Luna

FRANK LAMPARD

The Chelsea and England midfield giant has a Spanish partner, Elen Rives, so they named their daughter after the Spanish for 'moon'. David and Victoria Beckham had already earmarked it if they had a daughter. Doubt they're over the moon.

Should have considered: *Not upsetting the skipper*

Lux

BOBBY GILLESPIE

Nope, not a tribute to a soap. In Latin, 'lux' means 'light'. Which doesn't explain why the Primal Scream singer picked it, but there it is.

Should have considered: *Dove*

Blooming kids

Children with names from nature

Apple   GWYNETH PALTROW & CHRIS MARTIN

Bamboo   BIG BOI

Blossom   KACEY AINSWORTH

Carmen   ROBERT PLANT

Clementine   CLAUDIA SCHIFFER & MATTHEW VAUGHN

Daisy Boo   JAMIE OLIVER

Dandelion   KEITH RICHARDS

Fuschia   STING

Iris   SADIE FROST & JUDE LAW

Jessamine   PAUL WELLER

Lily-Rose Melody   JOHNNY DEPP & VANESSA PARADIS

Lilyella   MELANIE BLATT

Mathilda Plum   MOON UNIT ZAPPA

Peaches Honeyblossom   BOB GELDOF & PAULA YATES

Pepper   GRAHAM COXON

Poppy Honey   JAMIE OLIVER

Rosebud   PETER GREEN

Saffron Sahara   SIMON & YASMIN LE BON

Tallulah Lilac   JESSIE WALLACE

Tatjana Orchid   NICK RHODES

M

FROM *Mabel* TO *Moxie*

Mabel

TRACEY ULLMAN

OK, not that unusual … unless you're under 60. This is a French name meaning 'my fair maid' – and was a nice traditional choice by the British comedienne.

Should have considered: Ethel

Mackenzie

J K ROWLING

Scottish name meaning 'son of the fair-skinned' and therefore usually for boys. But the *Harry Potter* author (real name Joanne) says she and her GP hubby 'just really liked it'. And why not?

Should have considered: Voldemort

Maddox

ANGELINA JOLIE & BILLY BOB THORNTON

Whether they knew it or not, the *Tomb Raider* star and her then husband handed a Welsh name meaning 'beneficent' to the Cambodian orphan they adopted. SEE ALSO: *Zahara Marley*.

Should have considered: Pitt

Madison

ROBBIE FOWLER

Despite meaning 'son of a mighty warrior', it's one of the most popular girls' names in the US – and we suspect the Man City star wanted an 'American' name after David Beckham bagged Brooklyn. No suggestion that Robbie conceived her at Madison Square Garden.

Should have considered: Bronx

Maesa

BILL PULLMAN

Mysterious creation from the *Independence Day* star, especially since his sons have ordinary names. It's frankly amaesing.

Should have considered: Pushman

Makena'lei

HELEN HUNT

Makena'lei is named after a town in Hawaii. Since we don't know why, and Helen isn't saying, that's As Good As It Gets.

> ***Should have considered:*** *Honolulu*

Malu Valentine

DAVID BYRNE

Malu is another Hawaiian word, meaning 'peacefulness'. The Talking Heads frontman combined this with a Latin word for 'strong'.

> ***Should have considered:*** *Thirdegree*

Mandisa

DANNY GLOVER

Simple, this one ... the African-American star picked the Swahili word for 'sweet'.

> ***Should have considered:*** *Boxing*

Mandla Kadjay Carl

STEVIE WONDER

The first name of the Motown superstar's seventh child is Zulu for 'powerful and defiant'. The second is Swahili for 'born from God'. Carl means 'manly'. Mandla's surname is Stevie's real one, Morris. SEE ALSO: *Kailand.*

> ***Should have considered:*** *Johnny*

Manzie Tio

WOODY ALLEN & SOON-YI PREVIN

The film-making genius's second adopted daughter with Soon-Yi was named after Manzie Johnson, jazz drummer for clarinet legend Sidney Bechet (after whom the couple's first daughter was named).

> ***Should have considered:*** *Ellington*

Margaux

LORRAINE BRACCO

The *Goodfellas* star, also the shrink in *The Sopranos*, wed a Frenchman in the 1970s, hence the French name. It's a diminutive of Marguerite, meaning 'pearl'.

Should have considered: *Henrietta Hilary*

Marina Pearl

MATT LEBLANC & MELISSA McKNIGHT

Marina means 'of the sea'. So Joey from *Friends* has named his daughter 'pearl of the sea'. Which makes Melissa mother of pearl.

Should have considered: *Coral*

Marquise

50 CENT

The rapper, real name Curtis James Jackson, picked an odd one here. Perhaps he's unaware it's a title for a French noblewoman. Or maybe Mr Cent's little lad was intense, geddit?

Should have considered: *Bivouac*

Martha Sky Hope

ULRIKA JONSSON

Beautiful, optimistic name from the TV girl. Martha is a Biblical name meaning 'lady'. Sky is the upper atmosphere, seen from the Earth's surface. And hope is, of course, the thing with feathers that perches in the soul. SEE ALSO: *Bo*.

Should have considered: *Rose-Tint*

Mason

KELSEY GRAMMER

The name picked by the *Cheers* and *Frasier* star means 'stone-worker', as you might expect. SEE ALSO: *Greer*.

Should have considered: *Sloppy*

Mateo

COLIN FIRTH & LIVIA GIUGGIOLI

Another cool Mediterranean name from the *Pride and Prejudice* star and his Italian wife. It means 'devoted to God'. SEE ALSO: *Luca*.

Should have considered: Collina

Mateo Bravery

BENJAMIN BRATT & TALISA SOTO

TV's *Law and Order* star – long-time love of Julia Roberts – and his actress wife handed their son a lot to live up to with his middle name. Mateo will need every ounce of that courage when school-mates discover it.

Should have considered: Little

Mathilda Plum

MOON UNIT ZAPPA

When mum's Moon Unit, you might fear the worst for your own name. But Mathilda escaped lightly. Hers is an old German moniker meaning 'mighty in battle'. So she's a warlike fruit.

Should have considered: Mars Mission

Mattea Angel

MIRA SORVINO

The first is an obscure Hebrew name meaning God's gift – picked by the Oscar-winning actress (daughter of *Goodfellas*' Paul).

Should have considered: Aphrodite

Maya

UMA THURMAN & ETHAN HAWKE

There are dozens of meanings for Maya – she was Buddha's mum. It is also a Hindu word describing a form of the Goddess Devi. Uma played a character called Maya two years before her daughter was born. Maybe it's as simple as that. SEE ALSO: *Levon Roan*.

Should have considered: Mia

McCanna

The *Forrest Gump* and *Green Mile* star presumably named his boy after someone inspirational but it's not clear who. One thing though … a Scotsman with an inability to sneeze might exclaim 'McCanna Sinise!' … let's move on.

Should have considered: *Amgunna*

Memphis

BONO

The U2 frontman, really Paul Hewson, and his band have a strong connection with Memphis, Tennessee – home of the blues and rock 'n' roll, recording the album *Rattle and Hum* there in the late 1980s, shortly before the birth of Bono's daughter. SEE ALSO: *Elijah Patricius Bob Guggi Q.*

Should have considered: *BeBe*

Mercedes

VAL KILMER & JOANNE WHALLEY

Sure, it's a German car. But the firm's name derives from a major Austrian dealer in the early 1900s who rebranded Daimlers under his daughter's name Mercedes. It means 'mercy' in Spanish.

Should have considered: *Minnie*

Messiah

ALLEN IVERSON

Not much to live up to here for the daughter of the basketball star with the Philadelphia 76ers. There may be raised eyebrows when she walks into a business meeting with 'Messiah' on her name tag. The word, of course, means 'saviour'.

Should have considered: *Holly Spirit*

Mikaela

STEVEN SPIELBERG & KATE CAPSHAW

The great director of *ET* and *Schindler's List* picked the female form of Michael, though this is strictly speaking its Swedish form, with a 'k' instead of a 'ch'. SEE ALSO: *Destry, Sawyer*.

Should have considered: *Indiana*

Miller

STELLA McCARTNEY

Coincidence, presumably, that the fashion-designing Beatle's daughter should choose Miller, a name meaning 'he who mills'. She's named after a designer lager ... and so's he!

Should have considered: *Becks*

Milo

LIV TYLER

Cute name from the *Lord of the Rings* actress, daughter of Aerosmith singer Steve. It means 'merciful'.

Should have considered: *Aragorn*

Mingus

HELENA CHRISTENSEN

Mingus has no obvious meaning, so we presume the Danish supermodel, who likes dating musicians, paid tribute to Charlie Mingus, the jazz bandleader and composer.

Should have considered: *Parker*

Mirage

ERIC BURDON

Even allowing for the fact it was 1974, this is a peculiar name for the Animals singer to saddle a kid with. What was he thinking? Did she disappear when he approached?

Should have considered: *Phantom*

Missy

DAMON ALBARN

The Blur frontman's daughter is said to have been named after hip-hopper Missy Elliott (real name Melissa Arnette Elliott). And let's face it, it is a bit of a rap name.

Should have considered: *Lil Kim*

Misty Kyd

SHARLEEN SPITERI

Truly bonkers name from the singer with Texas. Misty was apparently named after the Clint Eastwood stalker movie *Play Misty for Me*. And Kyd because, presumably, she is one.

Should have considered: *Josie Wales*

Montana

RICHARD THOMAS

If you're picking US states to name your kids, you'd have thought John Boy Walton might have picked Virginia. Though his son's unlikely to have thanked him for that.

Should have considered: *Jim Bob*

Moon Unit

FRANK ZAPPA

Regularly tops polls of the weirdest celebrity names (though perhaps voters are unaware of Pilot Inspektor Lee). 'Moon' is potty enough. 'Unit' was apparently added because Frank thought her birth made him and his wife a family unit. Asked later why he gave his kids such bizarre names, the eccentric rocker explained: 'I wanted to.' SEE ALSO: *Ahmet, Diva Muffin, Dweezil.*

Should have considered: *What he was starting*

Morgan

CLINT EASTWOOD

Welsh name meaning 'bright'. Can it be a coincidence Clint's co-star in his two most Oscar-laden movies (*Unforgiven* and *Million Dollar Baby*) was Morgan Freeman? Probably.

Should have considered: *Harriet Callahan*

Morgana

MORGAN FREEMAN

See previous entry. Can it be a coincidence that her father is Morgan Freeman? Absolutely not. SEE ALSO: *Alphonse, Deena, Saifoulaye*.

Should have considered: *Clinta*

Moses Amadeus

WOODY ALLEN & MIA FARROW

The movie-maker's adopted son was not named after the recipient of the Ten Commandments. He was named after Moses Malone, a brilliant NBA basketball player for 20 years until the mid-1990s. Woody's Moses apparently shares a birthday with Mozart, hence Amadeus. See 'Mamma Mia', on page 173, for a list of all Mia Farrow's children.

Should have considered: *Meadowlark*

Moxie CrimeFighter

PENN JILLETTE

The American comic/magician played an idiotic trick on his daughter here. He justified it thus: 'When she's pulled over for speeding she can say, "But officer, we're on the same side. My middle name is CrimeFighter".'

Should have considered: *Her sanity*

N

FROM *Najee* TO *Noah*

Najee

LL COOL J

Najee Rashid is a jazz sax and flute player who has dabbled with hip-hop – maybe he was the inspiration for the rapper (real name James Todd Smith). SEE ALSO: *Italia, Samaria*.

Should have considered: *Marsalis*

Natalia Diamante

KOBE BRYANT

The LA Lakers basketball legend, middle name Bean, picked an Italian first name meaning 'born at Christmas', which she nearly was (19 January 2003). Diamante is a small, glittering ornament.

Should have considered: *Hooper*

Navarone

PRISCILLA PRESLEY

The son Elvis's wife had with lover Marco Garibaldi is named after an island off Turkey. It's known only for the war movie *The Guns of Navarone*. Presumably Priscilla thought it sounded cool.

Should have considered: *Iwo Jima*

Nell Marmalade

HELEN BAXENDALE

Bonkers offering from the *Cold Feet* and *Friends* actress. Nell is a diminutive of Helen, Greek for 'bright one'. Marmalade is for spreading on toast, not your kids.

Should have considered: *Toasten Honey*

Nevis

NELLY FURTADO

The meaning of Nevis is unclear, but Ben Nevis in Scotland is the tallest mountain in the British Isles, at 1,344 m (4,409 ft). Maybe the 'Like a Bird' singer's daughter is very tall.

Should have considered: *K2*

Nicklaus Caledonia

GLEN CAMPBELL

The Rhinestone Cowboy singer is a keen golfer and seems to have honoured golfing legend Jack Nicklaus. Possibly coincidentally, Caledonia is a course in South Carolina. SEE ALSO: *Shannon*.

Should have considered: *Tiger Carnoustie*

Noah

THOM YORKE

Radiohead's frontman plucked his son's excellent name from the Old Testament and writes that he hopes the youngster, in the event of a catastrophic flood, will build an ark and sail folk to the moon. Good luck with that. SEE ALSO: *Agnes*.

Should have considered: *Kid A*

FROM *Ocean* TO *O'Shea*

Ocean

The *Bird* movie star is big on nature names. But then he is a Forest. We imagine Ocean as a big lad who's a bit wet, but that may be a touch unfair. SEE ALSO: *Autumn, Sonnet, True*.

Should have considered: Woody

Oriole Nebula

DONOVAN

The spaced-out songwriter who gave us daughter Astrella Celeste conjures up another name of intergalactic daftness. An oriole is a tropical bird. A nebula is a mass of space dust or gas. SEE ALSO: *Astrella Celeste, Ione Skye*.

Should have considered: Warbler Supernova

O'Shea

ICE CUBE

Sadly not a tribute to Manchester United star John O'Shea … the rapper and movie actor was born O'Shea Jackson (NOT O'Shea Cube) and named his son O'Shea Jr.

Should have considered: Rubik

P

FROM *Paige* TO *Puma*

Paige Carlyle

RON HOWARD

Paige is French for 'attendant'. Carlyle is for New York's Hotel Carlyle, where the *Happy Days* star/*Beautiful Mind* director conceived her. SEE ALSO: *Bryce Dallas, Reed*.

Should have considered: *Paige Waldorf*

Paloma

EMILIO ESTEVEZ

The *Young Guns* actor, son of *West Wing* star Martin Sheen, has a Spanish grandad and is proud of his roots, choosing the Spanish word for 'dove'.

Should have considered: *Paella*

Paris Michael

MICHAEL JACKSON & DEBBIE ROWE

Jacko lived in France in the late 1990s and conceived his daughter in Paris. His then wife Debbie insisted she was also called Michael. Despite the divorce, they'll always have Paris. SEE ALSO: *Prince Michael, Prince Michael II*.

Should have considered: *Calais Michael*

Parker

FAY RIPLEY

No, she's not named after Lady Penelope's butler in *Thunderbirds*. Some friends of the *Cold Feet* star called their kid Ripley – so in a conversation about giving children a surname for a first name, Fay joked she would use THEIR name if she sprogged. And she did.

Should have considered: *Baxendale*

Peaches Honeyblossom

BOB GELDOF & PAULA YATES

Ammunition here for those who say exotic names expose kids to ridicule … Peaches claims she was teased mercilessly about hers at school (see 'You've got to be kidding', page 133). SEE ALSO: *Fifi Trixibelle, Pixie, Heavenly Hiraani Tiger Lily.*

> ***Should have considered:*** *Kumquat*

Pearl

MEAT LOAF

You'd think the 'Bat out of Hell' star might have considered Sliced or Wholemeal. But his daughter refuses to be a Loaf and uses his original surname (he's Marvin Aday in reality).

> ***Should have considered:*** *Anapple, Amars*

Pedro

FRANCES McDORMAND & JOEL COEN

The brilliant *Fargo* actress and her director husband adopted a boy from Paraguay, hence the Spanish word for 'rock'.

> ***Should have considered:*** *Barton Fink*

Pepper

GRAHAM COXON

The ex-Blur guitarist presumably wished to convey a fiery temperament with this popular condiment.

> ***Should have considered:*** *Chilli*

Persia

GARY NUMAN

The second daughter of the electro-pop pioneer (real name Gary Webb) cops the old name for Iran – the choice of his missus, apparently. Are you completely Shah, dear? SEE ALSO: Raven.

> ***Should have considered:*** *Worldwide*

Phinnaeus

JULIA ROBERTS & DANNY MODER

The Pretty Woman's choice has a certain something. The 'usual' spelling is Phineas – meaning 'oracle' in Greek myth. There is even a Biblical warrior called Phinehas. The great American showman P T Barnum was Phineas. But what Julia and her movie cameraman hubby's motive was is unknown.

Should have considered: *Yoda*

Phoenix Chi

MEL B

Scary Spice Melanie Brown explained that the Chinese believe Chi is an energy in all living things. Meanwhile the phoenix is a mythical creature said to die in flames before being reborn in the ashes. Something her pop career hasn't achieved.

Should have considered: *Unicorn*

Pilot Inspektor

JASON LEE

Perhaps the maddest name of all. The star of movies *Chasing Amy* and *Stealing Harvard* was apparently inspired by a song from indie band Grandaddy called 'He's Simple, He's Dumb, He's The Pilot' (a nice compliment to the poor lad, for starters). So what IS a pilot inspector? A gasman who inspects pilot lights? An airline official who checks pilots? And how about that 'k' as Jason's *piece de resistance*? Presumably so the boy can stand out from all the other Pilots Inspector.

Should have considered: *Professional help*

Piper Maru

GILLIAN ANDERSON

I'm Piper Maru … how do you do? We don't know why the *X Files* beauty picked Piper. Peter Piper famously picked a peck of pickled pepper. But we digress. Maru is Polynesian for 'gentle'.

Should have considered: *Scully*

Pirate
JONATHAN DAVIS

Excellent! Brand your kid a criminal at birth! The vocalist with hard rockers Korn presumably wants the boy to wear hoop earrings and storm ships brandishing a cutlass. He'll probably become a teacher.

Should have considered: *Mugger*

Pixie
BOB GELDOF & PAULA YATES

How does she feel being named after the mischievous, pointy-eared, green-jacketed little people of English folklore? Does she, like sister Peaches, consider her name Poxie? SEE ALSO: *Fifi Trixibelle, Peaches Honeyblossom, Heavenly Hiraani Tiger Lily.*

Should have considered: *Imp*

Poppy Honey
JAMIE OLIVER

The Naked Chef's first daughter's name comprises two handy ingredients for baking – honey and poppy seeds. SEE ALSO: *Daisy Boo.*

Should have considered: *Sesame Cinnamon*

Presley
CINDY CRAWFORD & RANDE GERBER

The word means 'from the priest's land' – but The King must be the motive behind the supermodel's choice. Indeed, her son has been nicknamed Elvis from an early age. SEE ALSO: *Kaia Jordan.*

Should have considered: *Lewis, Vincent*

Prince Michael
MICHAEL JACKSON & DEBBIE ROWE

No, it wasn't a faux royal title. Nor a tribute to his pop rival Prince. The reason was that Jacko's grandfather and great-grandfather were called Prince. SEE ALSO: *Paris Michael, Prince Michael II.*

Should have considered: *Jesse*

Prince Michael II

MICHAEL JACKSON &
DEBBIE ROWE

Two seconds' thought went into thinking up this sequel. Jacko further put his second son on the map by insisting on calling the boy Blanket and dangling him from a fifth-floor hotel balcony. SEE ALSO: *Paris Michael, Prince Michael*.

Should have considered: *Sticking with Prince Michael II*

Puma

ERYKAH BADU

Note to Erykah – a soul singer – a puma is a big cat native to North and South America. It is not a baby girl's name, unless you want her to grow up savage and eat raw meat.

Should have considered: *Kitty*

You've got to be kidding

The celebrity children who rebelled

Sometimes the children of stars are proud of their exotic names. Sometimes they're very definitely not. See how this lot reacted:

Dandelion Richards

Dandelion Richards rejected her dad Keith's rock 'n' roll lifestyle – as well as the hippy name he gave her. The daughter of the Rolling Stones guitarist and model Anita Pallenberg was born on 17 April 1972 in Geneva, Switzerland, and seems to have been named after a song written in 1967 by Richards and Mick Jagger.

She was brought up by Keith's mum Doris, away from the madness surrounding the Stones' lifestyle. By the time she was a teenager she had dumped Dandelion and opted for the more sober Angela, becoming known as Angie.

In 1999 she married a carpenter and now leads a quiet life in Dartford, Kent, well away from the spotlight other Rolling Stones kids find themselves in. She is reportedly teetotal … not a word often used in the same sentence as any mention of her dad.

Free Carradine

Hippy actors David Carradine and Barbara Hershey presumably wanted their newborn son to be a free spirit when he was born in 1972. So they named him Free. Free Carradine, that is. Had he been Free Hershey, American magazines might have wanted to give him away on the front cover.

In the end there was only one thing from which Free wished to be free. Yes, you've guessed it … his hippy forename. So Free became Tom.

Peaches Honeyblossom Geldof

Peaches Geldof stuck with her name – but has some harsh words to say about it. She and sisters Fifi Trixibelle, Pixie and half-sister Heavenly Hiraani Tiger Lily are saddled with some of the dafter monikers concocted by the stars.

Peaches reckons her name has haunted her all her life:

'I am named after a fruit,' she says. 'I'm not Jane or Sarah or Samantha, I am Peaches.

'At primary school I got teased a lot, just as little Apple Martin [Gwyneth Paltrow and Chris Martin's daughter] will.

'The most common taunt was, "Oi, Peaches, are your parents bananas?"

'Every Tuesday we were served sliced peaches. Every time I dared to raise my spoon, jubilant cries of "You're eating yourself!" would echo around the room.

'Then again, I was going to be called Angel Delight [an instant dessert] at one point, so I suppose I can count myself lucky.'

Rolan Bolan

One rock star child used his barmy name to his advantage –
and would never dream of changing it.

Glam rock legend Marc Bolan aped his close friend David
Bowie by saddling his son with a rhyme. The poor lad, born in
1975, became Rolan Bolan.

But Rolan reacted very differently from Zowie Bowie
(see page 139). He explained: 'One night David, my dad and
their producer Tony Visconti were sitting around discussing
children's names. Bowie had called his son Zowie Bowie, so
Dad said he'd call me Rolan Bolan. That's how my name came
about and I'm proud of it. I throw it around every chance I get.

'It gave me a sense of humour. If people laughed, I laughed
with them. It was the name my dad gave me and it will do
for me.'

Satchel Farrow

Woody Allen and Mia Farrow named their son Satchel at the film-maker's insistence. It was a tribute to Leroy 'Satchel' Paige, a black baseball pitcher who spent most of his career during the 1920s, '30s and '40s in the so-called Negro Leagues, excluded from the big time by racism. By the time he made his debut for a top-flight club he was 42 and past his prime – but still a match-winner. 'Satchel Paige was a hero of mine,' says Woody.

Woody's Satchel was born in 1987. By the time he was seven he had been so badly teased about his name at school he changed it to Seamus. Mia says: 'The children at school were kidding him. A satchel is a thing that is carried. Seamus is the Irish name for James. It is much better.'

Woody wasn't in much of a position to argue – he and Mia had split up. Seamus doesn't seem to have any emotional baggage from being a Satchel – he's a well-adjusted brainbox who started college at 11 and was accepted into Yale Law School at 16.

Zowie Bowie

Zowie Bowie was saddled with a comical rhyming name –
but with his dad David about to reinvent himself as Ziggy
Stardust, it could have been worse. Nonetheless Zowie was
too much for the boy, who became Joe, and later Duncan.

He was actually born Duncan Zowie Jones in 1971 –
but became simply Zowie Bowie, apparently on the insistence
of the rock star's first wife Angie. She chose the name Zoe
because it's Greek for 'life', but changed the spelling so it
wouldn't be confused with a girl's name.

Zowie grew up with his dad after his parents split and by
the time he was sent to Gordonstoun public school in Scotland
he had become the anonymous Joe Jones – using his dad's
real surname. Level-headed Joe, who was shielded by his dad
from the excesses of rock and roll, got seven O-levels, went on
to A-levels and a philosophy degree in Ohio.

At some point after leaving school he changed his name
again, ditching Joe for his original Duncan. Nowadays he
steadfastly avoids the limelight and was last reported to have
taken a course at film school in London.

Q

FROM *Quincy* TO *Quinlan*

Quincy

DABNEY COLEMAN ☺

Tempting to think that the likeable movie and TV actor (from *Tootsie*, *9 to 5* and *On Golden Pond*) named his daughter after the 1970s TV series *Quincy*, involving a crime-busting coroner. And guess what … Dabney was in a couple of episodes!

> ***Should have considered:*** *Kojak*

Quinlan Dempsey

BEN STILLER ☺

The *Zoolander* and *Dodgeball* movie star picked an Irish name for 'fit and strong', plus a second name which is Gaelic for 'proud'.

> ***Should have considered:*** *Whisky De*

R

FROM *Racer* TO *Ryder*

Racer

ROBERT RODRIGUEZ

The hot young director of movies *Sin City* and *Once Upon a Time in Mexico* isn't afraid to gamble. What if Racer grows up to be a couch potato? SEE ALSO: *Rebel, Rocket*.

Should have considered: *Roddy*

Rafe

TIMOTHY SPALL

The star of *Harry Potter* and *The Last Samurai*, not to mention *Auf Wiedersehen, Pet*, picked a posh form of Ralph. And with a name like that, the lad was never going to be anything but an actor.

Should have considered: *Larry*

Rafferty

JUDE LAW & SADIE FROST

Rafferty means 'rich' – simple as that. And when your parents are Sadie and Jude (who reportedly got $10,000,000 for *Cold Mountain*) you probably don't need reminding. SEE ALSO: *Iris*.

Should have considered: *Denis*

Rain

RICHARD PRYOR

Actress Rain had a difficult upbringing, her comic genius father being prone to, ahem, excess. On top of all that he called her Rain. Pour thing.

Should have considered: *Sleet*

Rainey

ANDIE MACDOWELL

Gloomy old name to give a kid, her consolation being that if her *Four Weddings* star mum has saved for a rainy day, she's entitled to the lot.

Should have considered: *Sunny*

Ramona

TRE COOL

From Green Day, the champions of punk rock in the 1990s, a tribute to the inventors of punk rock in 1974, the Ramones. 'Ramona' is a song on their third album. Tre (in reality Frank Edwin Wright III) is a big fan. SEE ALSO: *Frankito*.

Should have considered: Sheena

Raphael

ROBERT DE NIRO

A Hebrew name meaning 'God has healed'. He may be named after the Renaissance painter. Or the *Goodfellas* star may just have liked it. And who's arguing?

Should have considered: Nero

Raven

GARY NUMAN

Not sure the first daughter of the 'Are Friends Electric' and 'Cars' singer wants to grow up to be a sinister-looking bird. What did you caw, caw me? SEE ALSO: *Persia*.

Should have considered: Robin

Rayna

MIKE TYSON

'Pure' and 'clean' aren't words associated with the ferocious heavy-weight but they're the meaning of the Hebrew name he gave his daughter. Probably best not to ask him about it.

Should have considered: Belle

Rebel

ROBERT RODRIGUEZ

Another risky one …what happens if Rebel, the movie director's boy, becomes an accountant? SEE ALSO: *Racer, Rocket*.

Should have considered: Colin, Philip

Rebop

TODD RUNDGREN

This was the name of Nigerian Rebop Kwaku Baah, once Eric Clapton's percussionist. Whether that's where Todd got it is anyone's guess.

Should have considered: Ginger

Redmond

FARRAH FAWCETT & RYAN O'NEAL

The wayward son of the *Charlie's Angels* star and the movie actor got a name meaning 'red-haired defender'. Sounds like Everton boss David Moyes in the old days.

Should have considered: Martin

Reed

RON HOWARD

His sisters are named after their places of conception, so you might imagine Reed was the product of a fumble on a river bank. Not so. His name simply means 'red-haired', which his dad, director of *A Beautiful Mind*, certainly was as Richie in *Happy Days*. Those days, and Ron's hair, are long gone. SEE ALSO: *Bryce Dallas, Paige Carlyle*.

Should have considered: Frankie

Regan

PAUL GASCOÍGNE & SHERYL KYLE

Gazza and Sheryl decided on this before the boy was born. Was the footballer a fan of Jack Regan in *The Sweeney*? Or of Ronald Reagan?

Should have considered: Bamber

Reignbeau

VING RHAMES

Marcellus Wallace in *Pulp Fiction* reckons this invention means 'to rule beautifully'. And he'll get 'medieval' on anyone who disagrees. SEE ALSO: *Freedom*.

Should have considered: Busta

Renee

Not a tribute to Renee and Renato, whose 'Save Your Love' was No. 1 in 1983. The singer was inspired by one of his favourite songs – The Four Tops' 'Walk Away Renee'.

Should have considered: *Maggie May*

Ripley

The British beauty from *Mission: Impossible II* picked a movie moniker – this is the surname of Sigourney Weaver's tough character in the *Alien* films.

Should have considered: *Ellen*

Roan

The adopted son of the *Basic Instinct* star is named after the Celtic word for a seal, about which magical tales were told in ancient mythology. Why? We don't know. SEE ALSO: *Laird Vonne*.

Should have considered: *Roland*

Rocco

Apparently Rocco – Italian for 'rest' – was decided on before he was born. The pop superstar's daughter Lourdes would run over to mum, kiss her bulge and say, 'Hello, baby Rocco'. *Lock, Stock* director Guy says Rocco was named after a relative. SEE ALSO: *Lourdes Maria*.

Should have considered: *Lionel*

Rocco Winchester

For Rocco, see above. Winchester has been a gun-makers since the late 1800s – and Ted, a rock legend who had a huge hit with 'Cat

Scratch Fever', is mad-keen on hunting. He wrote a cookbook subtly titled *Kill It and Grill It*. SEE ALSO: *Starr*.

> ***Should have considered:*** Smith, Wesson

Rocket ROBERT RODRIGUEZ

See also Racer and Rebel, the other sons of the *Sin City* movie director. Let's hope for Rocket's sake he doesn't come last in the sack race.

> ***Should have considered:*** Duzizbest

Roeg DONALD SUTHERLAND

The veteran Canadian star of *Kelly's Heroes*, *JFK* and many others paid tribute to Nicolas Roeg, director of his classic 1973 thriller *Don't Look Now*. SEE ALSO: *Rossif*.

> ***Should have considered:*** Altman

Roisin SINEAD O'CONNOR

The Irish singer of 'Nothing Compares 2 U' chose a name which may be unusual outside Ireland but has been in use there since the 16th century. It means 'little rose'. SEE ALSO: *Shane*.

> ***Should have considered:*** Hazel

Rolan MARC BOLAN

This quirky rhymer was the result of a late-night conversation with David Bowie (father of Zowie). (See entry in 'You've got to be kidding', page 137.)

> ***Should have considered:*** Tenpin

Roman

This, of course, means 'of Rome'. But it is unclear why *Lord of the Rings* star Cate picked it. Maybe after French director Roman Polanski? Or Chelsea boss Roman Abramovich? Perhaps not. SEE ALSO: *Dashiell*.

> ***Should have considered:*** *Frodo*

Roman

JOE PERRY

What was the Aerosmith guitarist thinking? Many fine names go with Perry. John, for instance. But not Roman.

> ***Should have considered:*** *Tom*

Romeo

DAVID & VICTORIA BECKHAM

It means 'pilgrim to Rome' and is, of course, most famous as the name of the doomed lover in Shakespeare's *Romeo and Juliet*. But the Bard wasn't the inspiration. Nor was the boy conceived in the back of an Alfa Romeo. 'It's just a name we love,' England football captain Becks revealed. SEE ALSO: *Brooklyn, Cruz*.

> ***Should have considered:*** *Falstaff*

Romeo Jon

JON BON JOVI

See above for meaning. This sounds more like a description of the rock singer in his wild younger days than his son's name.

> ***Should have considered:*** *Banjo*

Romey Marion

GABRIEL BYRNE & ELLEN BARKIN

This one, from the *Usual Suspects* star and his actress ex, is a short form of Rosemary. It also serves as an amusing adjective meaning 'like something found in Rome'. 'It's a bit Romey', one might say. And how we would laugh.

Should have considered: *Romesque, Romish*

Romy
ROB REINER

See previous entry. The actor and director of *When Harry Met Sally* and *This is Spinal Tap* has picked a minimalist variant, omitting the 'e'.

Should have considered: *Spearmint*

Rosebud
PETER GREEN

The Fleetwood Mac legend's choice is famously the dying word uttered by the newspaper tycoon in *Citizen Kane*, providing the mystery central to arguably the greatest movie of all time.

Should have considered: *Treesa*

Ross
DIANA ROSS

Fabulous though it would have been for the soul singer's boy to have been Ross Ross, he wasn't. Her husband, Ross's father, was Arne Naess, so he became Ross Arne Naess. Pity. SEE ALSO: *Chudney*.

Should have considered: *Naess*

Rossif
DONALD SUTHERLAND

Another director inspired the movie veteran when he named his second son … this time Frédéric Rossif. Their third son was Angus Redford, after Robert, who directed Sutherland in *Ordinary People*. SEE ALSO: *Roeg*.

Should have considered: *Pakula*

Roxy

MERCEDES RUEHL

The *Fisher King* star picked a diminutive of Roxana, the Persian name meaning 'dawn'.

Should have considered: *Mob*

Rufus Tiger

ROGER TAYLOR

Queen drummer chooses king's name: William II, son of William the Conqueror, was 'Rufus' due to his ruddy appearance (rufus is Latin for 'red-haired'). Tiger is inexplicable. And inexcusable.

Should have considered: *Ethelred*

Rumer Glenn

DEMI MOORE & BRUCE WILLIS

The oldest child of the movie couple (real names Demetria Guynes and Walter Bruce Willis) bagged an old English name meaning 'gipsy'. She is said to be named after English novelist Rumer Godden, though that could be just a rumour ... SEE ALSO: *Scout LaRue, Tallulah Belle.*

Should have considered: *Bob*

Ryder Russell

KATE HUDSON & CHRIS ROBINSON

Goldie Hawn's daughter married the Black Crowes singer – and named their son after the band's song 'Ryder', which made him leap about in her womb. Russell is after her stepdad, Kurt.

Should have considered: *Sugar Ray*

S

FROM *Saffron* TO *Sy'rai*

Saffron Sahara

SIMON & YASMIN LE BON

The Duran Duran singer and his model wife combined the orangey-yellow spice with the African desert. SEE ALSO: *Amber Rose, Tallulah Pine*.

Should have considered: Sandy

Sage Moonblood

SYLVESTER STALLONE

Highly pretentious faux Indian number from the *Rocky* star. Sage is a herb. The second name is baffling. SEE ALSO: *Seargeoh, Sistine*.

Should have considered: Basil

Saifoulaye

MORGAN FREEMAN

It may look a little like a Scrabble hand but the *Shawshank Redemption* star has picked a name meaning 'sword of truth' in Arabic. (Its Scrabble score is 16, by the way.) SEE ALSO: *Alphonse, Deena, Morgana*.

Should have considered: Soufflé

Sailor

CHRISTIE BRINKLEY

The supermodel reportedly chose this because she and her husband like sailing. Sailor's lucky they don't prefer staying in and playing Subbuteo.

Should have considered: Gardener

Salome

ALEX KINGSTON

The British *ER* actress chose a Biblical name meaning 'peace' – though the Bible's Salome was the dancing stepdaughter of Herod Antipas, who managed to get John the Baptist beheaded. Nice lass.

Should have considered: Delilah

Salvador

ED O'BRIEN

Not convinced about this Spanish-Irish combo from the Radiohead guitarist. Salvador Dali, yes. Ed O'Brien, yes. But Salvador O'Brien?

Should have considered: Conan

Sam Hurricane

DAVE STEWART & SIOBHAN FAHEY

No issue with Sam, of course. The second name was apparently for the Eurythmics star's favourite Bob Dylan song. SEE ALSO: *Django, Kaya.*

Should have considered: Blind Willie McTell

Samaria

LL COOL J

This is an ancient city, now in Jordan, said to be where John the Baptist is buried (see Salome). Whether the rap star, real name James Todd Smith, knew this is open to question. SEE ALSO: *Italia, Najee.*

Should have considered: Nablus

Satchel

WOODY ALLEN & MIA FARROW

Woody is wrongly thought to have named his son after jazz star Louis 'Satchmo' Armstrong (Satchmo being an abbreviation of Satchel Mouth). In fact, the sports-mad *Annie Hall* genius named him after baseball pitcher Leroy 'Satchel' Paige. Eventually, Satchel tired of being teased about being a bag and became Seamus (see page 138). See also page 173, for a list of Woody's and Mia's children.

Should have considered: Backpack

Satie

LOUIS GOSSETT JNR

A mystery, this, unless the *Officer and a Gentleman* star is a fan of French composer Erik Satie. SEE ALSO: *Sharron.*

Should have considered: Louis Jnr

Sawyer

STEVEN SPIELBERG & KATE CAPSHAW

What's the connection? The master movie storyteller and one of the great kids' stories of all time, Tom Sawyer? Must be it. SEE ALSO: *Destry, Mikaela*.

Should have considered: *Huck Finn*

Schuyler

MICHAEL J FOX

Pronounced 'sky-ler', it means 'shield' or 'shelter' in Dutch. Given that she is twin sister to Aquinnah (see separate entry) it probably wouldn't be a wild guess to say she may be named after one of the various Schuylers in New York State, where the *Back to the Future* star lives.

Should have considered: *Albany*

Scout LaRue

DEMI MOORE & BRUCE WILLIS

Scout was apparently named after Jean Louise 'Scout' Finch, young heroine of the Pulitzer Prize-winning novel *To Kill a Mockingbird*. And, we're guessing here, the second name is from Lash LaRue, legendary Western star. SEE ALSO: *Rumer Glenn, Tallulah Belle*.

Should have considered: *Freeman Hardy*

Sean Preston

BRITNEY SPEARS & KEVIN FEDERLINE

He was so nearly London. And his dad wanted Vegas. But in the battle of the place names, the winner was the Lancashire town, population 130,000. Was Britney swept up in Ashes fever during 2005 – naming the boy after Freddie Flintoff's birthplace?

Should have considered: *Wigan*

Seargeoh
SYLVESTER STALLONE

The *Rocky/Rambo* star's second son got an unusual derivative of Sergio, from the Latin for servant. Sly's version looks like an explosion in a vowel factory. SEE ALSO: *Sage Moonblood, Sistine*.

Should have considered: *Rambeoh*

Selah
LAURYN HILL

The Fugees singer picked a Hebrew name meaning 'pause and reflect'. She shifted 16 million copies of her solo album *The Miseducation of Lauryn Hill* … a big-Selah. Geddit? SEE ALSO: *Zion*.

Should have considered: *Primrose*

Seraphina
CHARLIE WATTS

This fancy number from the Rolling Stones' drummer is a Hebrew name deriving from Seraphim. The seraphim are, you may recall, God's highest-ranking angels.

Should have considered: *Angie*

Seven Sirius
ERYKAH BADU & ANDRE 3000

In a famous episode of the classic sitcom *Seinfeld*, George Costanza opines that the coolest name for a child is Seven. His pal Jerry Seinfeld replies: 'Yeah, I guess I could see it. Seven. Seven periods of school, seven beatings a day. Roughly seven stitches a beating, and eventually seven years to life. Yeah, you're doing that child quite a service.' Seems like hip-hop stars Erykah and Andre (from Outkast) sided with George. As for Sirius: you cannot be serious!

Should have considered: *Juan Tu*

Shane

Not an unusual name, of course – but notable for how the *Beverly Hills Cop* star, an African-American from Brooklyn, arrived at such a quintessentially Irish name. SEE ALSO: *Bria, Zola*.

Should have considered: *Brittany*

Shane

The Irish singer named her son after Pogues frontman Shane McGowan. Chances are the baby was born with more teeth. SEE ALSO: *Roisin*.

Should have considered: *Bono*

Shannon

A lovely Irish name meaning 'wise one', from the actor and country music legend. Ironically the Rhinestone Cowboy could have used a bit more wisdom in his own life. SEE ALSO: *Nicklaus Caledonia*.

Should have considered: *Alastair*

Shaquir

Second son of the LA Lakers basketball giant gets a derivative of, er, his dad's name. SEE ALSO: *Amirah, Shareef, Taahirah*.

Should have considered: *Ryan*

Shareef

His first son's in luck – in games of Cowboys and Indians he always gets to be the shareef. Oddly enough Shaq himself is a US deputy marshall, having gone through police training. SEE ALSO: *Amirah, Shaquir, Taahirah*.

Should have considered: *Marshall*

Sharron

LOUIS GOSSETT JNR

A perfectly normal name. If you're a girl, that is. This, however, is the son of the drill sergeant from *An Officer and a Gentlewoman*. Sorry, *Gentleman*. SEE ALSO: *Satie*.

Should have considered: *Tracie*

Shauna

ROBERT REDFORD

The veteran actor and director (*Butch Cassidy and the Sundance Kid*, *The Natural*, *Quiz Show*) picked a female derivative of Shaun, itself an Irish version of John, which means 'the Lord is gracious'.

Should have considered: *Roberta*

Shavaar

MS DYNAMITE

The Mercury Prize-winning rapper, real name Niomi McLean-Daley, chose the Persian word for 'prince'.

Should have considered: *Sticka*

Shawna

MICHAEL LANDON

See entry for Shauna. This name, from the star of *Little House on the Prairie*, is another variant of John. How often the phrase 'It's like a shawna in here' must have echoed around their house during hot summers.

Should have considered: *Shawnuff*

Shepherd Kellen

JERRY SEINFELD

The man behind one of TV's greatest comedies hasn't yet explained what inspired Shepherd. Or Kellen. Still, it earned him another laugh.

Should have considered: *Kramer*

Shooter

WAYLON JENNINGS 🙂

The country musician named his boy Waylon, but nicknamed him Shooter after he urinated on a nurse shortly after birth. Now he's simply Shooter Jennings.

Should have considered: *Peewee*

Sindri

BJÖRK 🙂

The quirky Icelandic singer's son got a name from Norse mythology. Sindri was a dwarf who made magical things for the gods. SEE ALSO: *Isadora*.

Should have considered: *Gimli*

Sistine

SYLVESTER STALLONE 🙂

In his spare time *Rocky/Rambo* is an oil painter, listing Leonardo Da Vinci as his hero. And presumably Sly was so taken with Michelangelo's work in the Vatican's Sistine Chapel he named his daughter after it. SEE ALSO: *Sage Moonblood, Seargeoh*.

Should have considered: *Mona Lisa*

Skylar

SHEENA EASTON 🙂

For its meaning see 'Schuyler'. We suspect it was just a name the Scottish '9 to 5' singer (real name Sheena Shirley Orr) fancied.

Should have considered: *Farr*

Sonnet

FOREST WHITAKER 🙂

A champion of hippy-era names, the *Bird* star named this daughter after the 14-line poems which date back to the 1200s. SEE ALSO: *Autumn, Ocean, True*.

Should have considered: *Limerick*

Sonny

SOPHIE ELLIS BEXTOR

The 'Murder on the Dance Floor' singer must have pondered hard for several moments before calling her son Sonny. Cute, though.

> ***Should have considered:*** *Boy*

Sonora

KELLY McGILLIS

The *Top Gun* and *Witness* star chose a Spanish name meaning 'pleasant sounding', which Sonora is. Hope she's not a snorer.

> ***Should have considered:*** *Senora*

Sophine

GENE SIMMONS

If you can't decide between Sophie and Josephine, here's the answer. It was good enough for the blood-spurting frontman from Kiss, always an arbiter of good taste.

> ***Should have considered:*** *Stephanine*

Sosie

KEVIN BACON & KYRA SEDGWICK

Sosie's a nice-sounding name from the *Mystic River* character actor and his actress wife. But when your surname's Bacon you have to be REALLY careful. And, sorry and all that, but Sosie Bacon still sounds like a crisp flavour. SEE ALSO: *Travis*.

> ***Should have considered:*** *Smokie*

Speck Wildhorse

JOHN MELLENCAMP

Utterly mad moniker rivalling Stallone's Sage Moonblood in the 'faux Indian' stakes. But then Mellencamp did once call himself John 'Cougar'. SEE ALSO: *Hud*.

> ***Should have considered:*** *Wolfchild Arrowhead*

Starlite Melody

MARISA BERENSON

The *Vogue* fashion model-turned-actress inflicted this on her daughter in the mid-1970s. What possessed her?

> ***Should have considered:*** *Moondust Symphonia*

Starr

TED NUGENT

Is the daughter of the heavy rocker and hunting fanatic named after Ringo? Or Bill Clinton's nemesis Kenneth? Almost certainly neither. Guess Ted just thinks she's a star. SEE ALSO: *Rocco Winchester*.

> ***Should have considered:*** *Planet*

Stellan

JENNIFER CONNELLY & PAUL BETTANY

The *Beautiful Mind* stars named their son after Bettany's friend, Swedish actor Stellan Skarsgard.

> ***Should have considered:*** *Crowe*

Storm Brieanne

NIKKI SIXX

Motley Crüe's bassist, real name Frank Carlton Serafino Ferranna, should expect misbehaviour with this dramatic choice. Put her and Rain Pryor together and run for cover. SEE ALSO: *Dekker, Gunner*.

> ***Should have considered:*** *Gail*

Story

GINUWINE

Fancy a story, Story? She is elder sister to Dream (see separate entry). And since the R 'n' B singer is actually Elgin Baylor Lumpkin, this makes them Dream Lumpkin and Story Lumpkin.

> ***Should have considered:*** *Dumpling*

Summer Song

An orphan adopted by Mia during the Vietnam war, she had greater problems to overcome than her name. But overcome that she did, becoming Daisy. See 'Wacky Families', page 173, for a list of Mia Farrow's children.

Should have considered: *Daisy*

Sy'rai

The R 'n' B star who had her own sitcom called *Moesha* (and whose real name is Brandy Rayana Norwood), says this name means 'princess'. 'She is a princess and I'm the queen,' she adds.

Should have considered: *Cognac*

T

FROM *Taahirah* TO *T'ziah*

Taahirah

SHAQUILLE O'NEAL

The 2.1m (7ft1in) basketball star chose an Arabic name meaning 'chaste'. Which is what Shaquille was … all over the court. Boom boom! SEE ALSO: *Amirah, Shaquir, Shareef.*

Should have considered: Tatum

Taj

STEVEN TYLER

This one, from Aerosmith's frontman, means 'crown' in Hindi. Tyler, father of movie star Liv, was originally Steven Victor Tallarico, by the way.

Should have considered: Rufus

Tali

ANNIE LENNOX

A short form of modern names Talicia or Talisa, but whether either inspired the Eurythmics star is unclear. Tali took Annie's tally of daughters to two.

Should have considered: Eurythmie

Tallulah Belle

DEMI MOORE & BRUCE WILLIS

One of the most up-and-coming celebrity girls' names – and the *Die Hard* and *Ghost* stars started the trend. It is said they named her after Jodie Foster's gangster's moll in the film *Bugsy Malone*. The most famous Tallulah was an actress – Tallulah Bankhead, born in 1902 and named after her gran, who in turn was named after Tallulah Falls, a waterfall in Georgia. The word 'Tallulah' is Choctaw Indian for 'leaping water'. But, oddly enough, it is also an Irish name meaning 'lady of abundance'. So now you're probably none the wiser. SEE ALSO: *Rumer Glenn, Scout LaRue.*

Should have considered: Niagara

Tallulah Grace
MICHAEL VAUGHAN 😊

See previous entry for Tallulah. England's cricket captain says he doesn't know what was behind Grace. But surely it must have been for W G Grace, the first real legend of English cricket?

    Should have considered: *Tallulah Botham*

Tallulah Lilac
JESSIE WALLACE 😊

The problem with this combo from *EastEnders*' Kat Slater – as with the Le Bons' choice (see next entry) – is that they sound like air fresheners.

    Should have considered: *Lavender Mist*

Tallulah Pine
SIMON & YASMIN LE BON 😊

Banish stale odours with a quick burst of Tallulah Pine – your room will smell like a forest on a spring morning. SEE ALSO: *Amber Rose, Saffron Sahara.*

    Should have considered: *Hawaiian Breeze*

Tamir
JONNY GREENWOOD 😊

The Radiohead lead guitarist's wife Sharona is Israeli – hence the Hebrew name meaning 'tall and wealthy'. Which describes his dad, too.

    Should have considered: *Pablo*

Tamla
SMOKEY ROBINSON 😊

The singing legend behind 'Tears of a Clown' and 'I Second That Emotion' (whose real name is William Robinson) named his daughter after his record label, Tamla/Motown.

    Should have considered: *MCA*

Tarian Nathaniel
TRAVIS TRITT

We'll let Travis, one of country music's biggest stars, explain: 'Tarian means strong and ambitious. And the pregnancy came as a surprise, so we chose the middle name Nathaniel because it means "gift from God".'

Should have considered: *Uppaclass*

Tarzana
LENE LOVICH

Well, the 'Lucky Number' pop singer was always eccentric – and her daughter's name (now just Taz) seems to be a female form of, er, Tarzan. SEE ALSO: *Valhalla*.

Should have considered: *Jane*

Tatjana Orchid
NICK RHODES

Duran Duran's keyboardist, real name Nick Bates, chose a Russian or Slavic name deriving from the Roman Tatianus, the meaning of which has been lost.

Should have considered: *Icy*

Tianie-Finn
DUNCAN JAMES

According to the Blue singer, this means 'bright star' in Irish.

Should have considered: *Etta*

Tiger Lily
ROGER TAYLOR

Cats galore in the Queen drummer's household. One son called Felix (a cartoon moggie), another called Rufus Tiger – and a daughter called Tiger Lily. And another daughter's called Rory Eleanor. Geddit? Roary! SEE ALSO: *Rufus Tiger*.

Should have considered: *Katia*

Travis KEVIN BACON & KYRA SEDGWICK

This offering, from the great movie actor and his wife, means 'crossing' in French, but it's popular in the US thanks to William Travis, heroic commander of the doomed Texan forces at the Alamo in 1836. SEE ALSO: *Sosie*.

> ***Should have considered:*** *Crockett*

Trilby BRUCE BERESFORD

Hats off to the *Driving Miss Daisy* director for scaling the peak of daftness with this one. She's presumably named after Trilby Comeaway, an Aborigine character in the Aussie's 1986 movie, *The Fringe Dwellers*.

> ***Should have considered:*** *Beret*

True Isabella Summer FOREST WHITAKER

She's the sister of Sonnet, and that's no lie. Another 'nature' pick from the star of *Panic Room*, among many others. SEE ALSO: *Autumn, Ocean, Sonnet*.

> ***Should have considered:*** *Winter Discontent*

Truman TOM HANKS

The world's most popular movie actor is a Democrat, and honoured 33rd President Harry S Truman.

> ***Should have considered:*** *Clinton*

Tryumph JAYSON WILLIAMS

This mad choice of the New Jersey Nets basketball ace is far from a triumph. SEE ALSO: *Whizdom*.

> ***Should have considered:*** *Vyktory*

Tu

ROB MORROW

See you Tu Morrow! At what point in the process of choosing a name did the star of TV's *Northern Exposure* and the movie *Quiz Show* decide the best thing was a gimmick based on his surname? Poor Tu is a prime candidate for a name change, if not today, then …

Should have considered: *The child's sanity*

Ty

WAYNE GRETZKY

The world's greatest ice hockey star picked a short form of Tyson, Tyler or Tyrone. Ty Cobb was one of baseball's greatest stars of all time.

Should have considered: *Puck*

Tyhamia

TIM MONTGOMERY

The meaning of this, from the great American sprinter, is unclear. It sounds like an ailment runners get through over-exertion.

Should have considered: *Diptheria*

Tyson

NENEH CHERRY

The hip-hop star behind 'Buffalo Stance' and 'Manchild' reportedly named her kid after boxer Mike Tyson, though he probably seemed more of a role model then as world champion than he does 17 years on! To make matters worse, the child in question is a girl.

Should have considered: *Lennox*

T'ziah

BUSTA RHYMES (TREVOR SMITH)

Not sure how the rapper pronounces this here.
Is it like 'desire', or is it 'tea's 'ere'?
Its meaning is unclear. Busta, give us a steer.

Should have considered: *Zabir Zaheer*

Wacky families

Sometimes, all the kids in a showbiz family have wacky names. Here's a selection of the most famous:

Mamma Mia

Mia Farrow's brood in full

With Andre Previn:

Matthew Phineas Previn

Sascha Villiers Previn

Fletcher Previn

Adopted with Previn:

Soon-Yi Previn

Lark Song Previn

Summer Song Previn, called Daisy

With Woody Allen:

Satchel, now Seamus

Adopted with Woody Allen:

Moses Amadeus

Dylan, later Eliza and then Malone

Further adopted kids:

Isaiah

Kaeli-Shea (now Quincy)

Gabriel Wilk (now Thaddeus)

Minh (now Frankie-Minh)

The Geldofs

Fifi Trixibelle
Peaches Honeyblossom
Pixie
and half-sister Heavenly Hiraani
    Tiger Lily

The Olivers

Daisy Boo
Poppy Honey

The Rosses

Betty Kitten
Harvey Kirby
Honey Kinney

The Whitakers

Autumn
Ocean
Sonnet
True

The Willises

Rumer Glenn
Scout LaRue
Tallulah Belle

The Zappas

Ahmet Emuukha Rodan

Diva Muffin

Dweezil

Moon Unit

Grandchild:

Mathilda Plum

V

FROM *Valentino* TO *Vance*

Valentino Luca

MELANIE SYKES

The TV presenter and Boddington's ad star chose a beautiful Italian name. After all, she's married to Italian actor Daniel Caltagirone.

Should have considered: *Calzone*

Valhalla

LENE LOVICH

The screechy-voiced 'Lucky Number' singer did her lad few favours naming him after the home for slain battle heroes of Norse myth. He could have become Val, but ended up as Hally. SEE ALSO: *Tarzana*.

Should have considered: *Valdoonican*

Vance

BILLY BALDWIN & CHYNNA PHILLIPS

The *Backdraft* star and his singer wife (from Wilson Phillips) picked an old English name meaning 'marshland'. Maybe they were swamped with possibilities. SEE ALSO: *Jameson Leon*.

Should have considered: *Boggie*

FROM *Walker* TO *Wynter*

Walker

JESSICA LANGE & SAM SHEPARD

Cool-sounding name from the *Tootsie/Cape Fear* actress and the supersmart playwright and actor. Not clear who the inspiration was. But how they must have punched the air in triumph when he took his first steps.

Should have considered: *Crawler*

Wallis

ANTHONY EDWARDS

Twin of Esme. Why Dr Greene from *ER* picked this is unknown. Highly unlikely to have been inspired by the most famous Wallis: Wallis Simpson – lover of King Edward VIII. SEE ALSO: *Bailey, Esme*.

Should have considered: *King*

Weston

NICOLAS CAGE

The *Leaving Las Vegas* star was born Nicholas Coppola but became Cage (after comic book character Luke Cage) to avoid living in the shadow of his famous uncle, *Godfather* director Francis. None of which explains Weston, old English for 'from the West town'. SEE ALSO: *Kal-El*.

Should have considered: *Bird*

Whizdom

JAYSON WILLIAMS

From the basketball star responsible for Tryumph, a sibling called Whizdom. And, wait for it, you have to doubt the wisdom of saddling the kid with that. Cheap gag, impossible to resist. SEE ALSO: *Tryumph*.

Should have considered: *Kunnyng*

Wilf

The *Cold Feet* star's choice is short-but-to-the-point and is a diminutive of Wilfred (which means 'much peace') or Wilford ('ford by the willows').

Should have considered: Chuck

Willard

Not an especially surprising choice from the star of *Men in Black* and *I, Robot*, when you consider he is Willard Smith Jnr and his dad Willard Sr. Will's son became Willard III, earning him the nickname 'Trey'. SEE ALSO: *Jaden Christopher Syre, Willow*.

Should have considered: Willard. Oh, he did.

Willem Wolfe

Willem is a Celtic contraction of the Rebel Yell rocker's first name (he's William Michael Albert Broad). As for Wolfe, let's hope he and Jerry Seinfeld's boy Shepherd never meet. SEE ALSO: *Bonnie Blue*.

Should have considered: Norfolk

Willie

Willie Hurt? See the nurse, boy! We assume the phrase doesn't mean the same in the States. And we pray the *Accidental Tourist* star never sends his boy to school in Britain … he'll never live it down, as it were.

Should have considered: Tuth

Willow Camille Reign

Willow is an embellishment of Will, as son Jaden is of Jada (see separate entry). As for Camille ('servant of the temple') and Reign

... they presumably just had a ring to them. SEE ALSO: *Jaden Christopher Syre, Willard*.

Should have considered: *Wilhelmina*

Wolfgang

EDDIE VAN HALEN

'Wolfie', as he is known, was named by his guitar maestro dad after another musical god, Wolfgang Amadeus Mozart.

Should have considered: *Ludwig*

Woody

ZOE BALL & NORMAN COOK

There was speculation that the TV star and the DJ/musician (Norman is, of course, Fatboy Slim) named their lad after Woody Allen, or Woody the nice-but-dim barman in *Cheers*. In fact, as a spokesman said: 'The name just appealed to them.'

Should have considered: *Captain*

Wyatt

KURT RUSSELL & GOLDIE HAWN

Tempting to think the man who played Wyatt Earp in *Tombstone* named his son after the Wild West lawman. Maybe so, but it was in 1986, long before the movie.

Should have considered: *Doc*

Wynter

TAWNY KITAEN

If you're going to name your daughter after a season, this is probably fourth choice. Perhaps the nubile actress – a veteran of Whitesnake videos (she married David Coverdale) and TV shows including *Seinfeld* – thought there were too many Summers and Autumns.

Should have considered: *Spryng*

Z

FROM *Zahara* TO *Zuleika*

Zahara Marley

ANGELINA JOLIE

The star of *Mr and Mrs Smith* and *Lara Croft* adopted this AIDS orphan in Ethiopia. Her first name means 'flower' in Swahili. The second is thought to be after reggae legend Bob – his son David 'Ziggy' Marley co-starred with Angelina as voice artists on *Shark Tale*. SEE ALSO: *Maddox*.

Should have considered: Dom

Zahra Savannah

CHRIS ROCK

For Zahra, see Zahara above. Savannah, chosen by the Oscars night comic, is Spanish for 'grassless plain'. SEE ALSO: *Lola Simone*.

Should have considered: Brighton

Zak

RINGO STARR

The Beatles drummer (Richard Starkey) picked out a 'cool' short form of Isaac, Hebrew for 'laughter'.

Should have considered: Khaki

Zelda

ROBIN WILLIAMS

Probably the only name in the book honouring a video game character, this was reportedly chosen by the Oscar-winning *Good Morning, Vietnam* actor because first son Zachary was obsessed with 'The Legend of Zelda'. That's a Nintendo game launched in 1986. The name itself derives from Griselda, German for 'dark battle'.

Should have considered: Mario

Zen

COREY FELDMAN

The former child star of *The Goonies* and *Stand By Me* named his son after the branch of Buddhism that leans heavily on meditation, leading to enlightenment. We wondered what Corey had been doing all these years.

Should have considered: *Mantra*

Zion   LAURYN HILL 😊

Having chosen a Hebrew name for her daughter, the Fugees singer picked the term for the promised land. Zion is her son with Bob Marley's boy Rohan. SEE ALSO: *Selah*.

Should have considered: *Jacob*

Zola   EDDIE MURPHY 😊

A few Zolas might have inspired the *Beverly Hills Cop* star: French novelist Emile Zola; Olympic runner Zola Budd; or Chelsea legend Gianfranco Zola. The name itself means 'lump of earth' in Italian. Zola will be pleased. SEE ALSO: *Bria, Shane*.

Should have considered: *Muddy*

Zowie   DAVID BOWIE 😊

Actually born Duncan Zowie, his mother insisted on him being called by the second name, which he very soon got fed up with. (See his entry in 'You've got to be kidding', page 139).

Should have considered: *Wowee*

Zuleika   CHARLES BRONSON 😊

The tough-guy actor (real name Charles Dennis Buchinski) – an American of Polish descent who starred in *The Great Escape* and *Deathwish* – chose a Persian name meaning 'brilliant beauty' for his daughter. And if anyone teased her, he shot them.

Should have considered: *Bronwen*

It could be worse

Even the maddest of celebs cannot match this: A Swedish couple went to court to fight for the right to name their son *Brfxxccxxmnpcccclllmmnprxvclmnckssqlbblll6*. It was a 'pregnant, expressionistic development that we see as an artistic creation'. However, for ease, they intended to pronounce it 'Albin'. A judge ruled against them.

Thanks to Martin Toseland and Isabel Sheehy at HarperCollins, and to the many books and websites which provided meanings and motivations behind the names.